SpringerBriefs in Law

AF798799

SpringerBriefs present concise summaries of cutting-edge research and practical applications across a wide spectrum of fields. Featuring compact volumes of 50 to 125 pages, the series covers a range of content from professional to academic. Typical topics might include: • A timely report of state-of-the art analytical techniques • A bridge between new research results, as published in journal articles, and a contextual literature review • A snapshot of a hot or emerging topic • A presentation of core concepts that students must understand in order to make independent contributions SpringerBriefs in Law showcase emerging theory, empirical research, and practical application in Law from a global author community. SpringerBriefs are characterized by fast, global electronic dissemination, standard publishing contracts, standardized manuscript preparation and formatting guidelines, and expedited production schedules

More information about this series at http://www.springer.com/series/10164

Charles Foster • Jonathan Herring

The Law as a Moral Agent

Making People Good

Springer

Charles Foster
Faculty of Law
University of Oxford
Oxford, UK

Jonathan Herring
Faculty of Law
University of Oxford
Oxford, UK

ISSN 2192-855X ISSN 2192-8568 (electronic)
SpringerBriefs in Law
ISBN 978-3-030-71333-1 ISBN 978-3-030-71334-8 (eBook)
https://doi.org/10.1007/978-3-030-71334-8

© The Author(s), under exclusive license to Springer Nature Switzerland AG 2021
This work is subject to copyright. All rights are solely and exclusively licensed by the Publisher, whether the whole or part of the material is concerned, specifically the rights of translation, reprinting, reuse of illustrations, recitation, broadcasting, reproduction on microfilms or in any other physical way, and transmission or information storage and retrieval, electronic adaptation, computer software, or by similar or dissimilar methodology now known or hereafter developed.
The use of general descriptive names, registered names, trademarks, service marks, etc. in this publication does not imply, even in the absence of a specific statement, that such names are exempt from the relevant protective laws and regulations and therefore free for general use.
The publisher, the authors, and the editors are safe to assume that the advice and information in this book are believed to be true and accurate at the date of publication. Neither the publisher nor the authors or the editors give a warranty, expressed or implied, with respect to the material contained herein or for any errors or omissions that may have been made. The publisher remains neutral with regard to jurisdictional claims in published maps and institutional affiliations.

This Springer imprint is published by the registered company Springer Nature Switzerland AG.
The registered company address is: Gewerbestrasse 11, 6330 Cham, Switzerland

Contents

Chapter 1
Introduction

Abstract This chapter introduces the themes of the book. Law is ubiquitous. It provides the sea we live in and the rules by which we live our lives. This chapter introduces the central theme of the book: the role of the law in making us good. As the law interferes significantly with liberty it requires a strong justification: making people *better* is a plausible justification.

Keywords Good · Society · Altruism · Identity · Murder

'The world is full of law', wrote the Israeli judge, Aharon Barak. It meant, for him, that there is nowhere to which the law does not reach. He intended it as a statement to buttress his high view of the rule of law, but many of us will find it threatening. We want there to be places that are entirely our own: our bedrooms, perhaps, or our bodies. And certainly our minds. We don't want to be told what we can and can't do with our bodies, and still less to be told what we can and can't think. Statements like Barak's, in the mouths of totalitarians with an agenda completely opposite to his, have been used to justify great evil. Even for those in the notionally free west, the strictures of the law often chafe.

As a description of the ubiquity of law, Barak's statement is correct. Usually, in the west, we don't *see* the law, just as fish, swimming all the time in water, presumably don't comment to themselves that they are wet. It is, we think, hard to say that freedom is the default position: that everything that is not prohibited is permitted—not because it does not accurately articulate the political philosophy of most of our lawmakers (it probably does—or at least did until recently)—but because the number of exceptions to the rule means that it is no rule at all. Where we can identify an apparently unfettered freedom, we are likely to see, when we examine it closely, that it is in fact hedged round with rules, or that it entails an inhibition of the freedom of others.

We see this from the very beginnings of human life to after its end.

I can have sexual intercourse, but only with someone who is capable of adopting a mental attitude towards the intercourse that is prescribed by the law, and who is over a particular age. I am not allowed to have sexual intercourse while my partner is

© The Author(s), under exclusive license to Springer Nature Switzerland AG 2021

C. Foster, J. Herring, *The Law as a Moral Agent*, SpringerBriefs in Law,
https://doi.org/10.1007/978-3-030-71334-8_1

under the influence of psilocybin mushrooms picked from the field next door because, the state says, those mushrooms will induce a state of mind which is inconsistent with membership of society, and in any event may make consent to the intercourse, in the sense mandatory for lawful intercourse, impossible.

If I am a fetus, I may, in England, be killed at any gestational age up to 24 weeks because, effectively, my mother does not want me, and if I have what the state regards as a serious disability, I can be killed at any point up to term. In neither case will I, or my father, have any right to make representations.

If I have a child, I will be required to register it, clothe it, feed it, and educate it in a way endorsed by the state. If I do not, I may find myself childless.

Throughout my life I will be required to toe the line set by the law. If my mental state does not accord with the state's view of normality, I may be deprived of my liberty and compulsorily treated. If I do not pay my taxes (perhaps because I think that they would be spent on immoral purposes), I may lose my house. If I buy a sandwich the purchase is governed by the rules of contract law. My sovereignty over my body, as a capacitous adult, is often said—typically in the context of discussions about the refusal of medical treatment—to be absolute, but there are many things that I cannot do. I cannot, for instance, consent to the infliction of serious bodily injury outside a medical context, even when (for example for sexual gratification) I might devoutly desire it. And whenever what I do with my body affects others, their considerations are taken into account in deciding what is legitimate for me. My ability to express myself by playing my electric guitar in the garden is restricted by the law of nuisance: my freedom to drive my car at the speed I want is constrained by the speed limit: my freedom to plunge a knife into my neighbour's heart is inhibited by the law of murder.

We are not protesting here about the propriety of these inhibitions. We would not want to live in an anarchy which had no law of murder. It is plainly right that sexual activity with children should be criminalised. And so on. Our only points are: first, that law is everywhere. And, second, that the law which is everywhere assumes some ethical norms. It assumes, for instance, that it is wrong to kill a person who has emerged from their mother's uterus.

It is a serious thing to interfere with someone's ability to live their life in exactly the way they want. And so law is a serious business. All laws need strenuous justification. That means that their normative presumptions must be clearly identified and interrogated. If, for instance, the rationale for an otherwise regrettable interference with my freedom is that it will increase the overall happiness of society, that needs to be understood. Yet it is very rare for the law to be so explicit.

This book is an attempt to see whether one possible objective of the law—to make individuals morally better—is in fact one of its objectives; and if it is, how the law sets out to realise the objective, and whether it should use different methods; and if it is not an objective, whether it should be.

We recognise that this cannot be solely a legal exercise. Indeed it might well be argued that these are essentially political questions, to do with the reach of the state, the terms of the social contract, and other ways of defining the place of the individual in society. Our justification for writing this book is that, very often, the philosophical and political devils are in the legal detail. It is all very well saying, abstractly, what it is acceptable to surrender in return for the privilege of citizenship. It is quite another to note how you feel when you read through a statute that mandates or forbids a particular kind of behaviour. Law is what happens when politics stops talking and starts to work. So we think that there is a real value in surveying the law to see what political philosophy actually *does*.

Barak is not the only one who thinks that the world is full of law. Many religions, thinking that nothing, even our most shameful, unvoiced thoughts, is hidden from God, believe that everything (including our thoughts) is subject to law which derives its substance from God's nature. Individual morality is central to all such conceptions. In the Judaeo-Christian tradition the reasoning goes something like this: divine law mandates individual morality because humans are made in God's image; God's edicts reflect His character; one therefore becomes more God-like by acting in accordance with those edicts; and because human character and God's character are at root similar, one will thrive best as a human if one acts in accordance with your real nature—which is also God's nature.

Many secular schemes of law, while abandoning this theological reasoning, come to similar conclusions. Legal strictures are made palatable by an appeal to individual thriving. You will be happier (says the law), if you obey the rules. That obedience will be easier if it proceeds from a constitutionally obedient, law-abiding character: inconsistency with oneself is exhausting, and indeed being true to oneself—being *authentic*—is one source, if not *the* source, of morality. You will be happiest if you are a Good Citizen whose authentic individual morality coincides with societal morality. The law might be pragmatically concerned mainly with actions, but good actions will be easier if you have the good thoughts that go naturally with them. The law, as we will see, is only rarely concerned directly with thoughts that are unaccompanied by actions—though it is often very interested in the mental states associated with actions: the whole notion of *mens rea* in criminal law is concerned with those states. But the law is often indirectly concerned with good and bad thoughts because they conduce to right action, good citizenship, the good of others, and societal stability. It is Good to be Good, the law declares in various ways.

Throughout this book we return constantly to a number of themes. Is it indeed good to be good? And if so for whom? And what is meant by 'good'? If altruism or empathy are at the core of morality, as some would insist, should individual altruism be encouraged by the law, even if it does not seem to be conducive to the objective good of the individual? What price can legitimately be demanded for membership of the club we call society? And who does the pricing? What is the relationship between good thinking and good doing? Can identity ever be part of the sum demanded for membership? Is society's only justification the enhancement of individuals?

We think that it is hard enough and important enough to identify a few of the right questions, and that is what we have sought to do. Answers would be dangerously hubristic, and so we haven't even attempted any.

Chapter 2
Contract and the Law of Property

Abstract This chapter explores the role of contract law in making us good. It explains how contract law ensures that we keep promises, provides a framework for people to work together in joint projects, and provides a mechanism for dealing with disputes between people. We emphasise that the success of contract law is not seen in the cases that come to court, but the extensive compliance with contractual obligations and the amicable resolution that occurs without recourse to the court. The law of property also provides a means of avoiding disputes over material objects and encourages people to invest time and effort in creation.

Keywords Contract · Property · Law and economics · Promises · Good faith · Commons

2.1 Introduction

It is a trite observation that private law affects many parts of our everyday lives. We enter contracts, exercise property rights or comply with our duties of care in the law of tort many times for most days of our lives. Yet few people will appear at a court in relation to such issues, unless they have the misfortune of being a litigation lawyer! In part this demonstrates the success of the legal regime. Contracts are normally complied with, and if they are not compensation is voluntarily paid. People respect each other's property rights and comply with duties of care. While to the lay person, the impact of law might be thought of in terms of dramatic court cases, in fact the real significance of the law is found in far more mundane compliance with legal obligations.

It is important, therefore, when considering the justification for or the role of private law not to focus simply on the idea of court-based remedies. They are an important part of the law, but only a small part. It is the role of the law in enabling and nudging people into complying with contractual obligations, into taking care to avoid harming others, and into respecting property rights, which is by the far more important part of the law.

© The Author(s), under exclusive license to Springer Nature Switzerland AG 2021

C. Foster, J. Herring, *The Law as a Moral Agent*, SpringerBriefs in Law,
https://doi.org/10.1007/978-3-030-71334-8_2

In this chapter we argue that the scaffolding of legal rights provided in private law (and particularly in the law of contract and that related to the ownership and disposition of property), which sets out agreed ways of behaviour between individuals, creates an environment in which doing good is encouraged. After this introduction to its themes the chapter will explore contract law and property law, using a number of examples.

2.2 Theories of Private Law

Before focussing on those specific areas more will be said about the nature of private law generally. Recently, there have been bold attempts to determine what private law is seeking to achieve. Very broadly we might break down the competing theories into five categories:

2.2.1 Law and Economics

Under this paradigm the aim of private law is to maximise wealth and economic efficiency. Eric Posner (2001) suggests that it is based on two assumptions:

(i) Individuals conform to the rationality assumptions of economic theory; and
(ii) Contract law promotes "efficiency"

As Posner (2001, p. 21) explains

> The first premise is that individuals have preferences over states of the world; that people's behavior conforms to their preferences; that these preferences are consistent and transitive; and that they can be represented as utility functions. In addition, people have high enough discount factors and find it worthwhile to invest in legal advice. Otherwise, the law would not affect people's behavior.

Nick McBride (2019, p. 72) has provided a powerful challenge to such an approach, developing a scenario imagined by Ronald Dworkin:

> Ronnie has a bowl of rice he is willing to sell. Derek, who is starving and poor and needs the rice to live, can only afford to offer Ronnie 50p for the bowl of rice. Amartya, who is very rich and fancies having the rice with his dinner, is willing to pay £10 for the bowl of rice out of his extensive riches. In 'Society 1' Ronnie takes pity on Derek and sells him the bowl of rice, thereby saving his life, and foregoing the extra £9.50 that he would have made selling the bowl of rice to Amartya. In 'Society 2' Ronnie sells the bowl of rice to Amartya. We can ask Dworkin's question again: Is there *any* respect in which Society 2 is superior to society 1? If the answer is 'no', then this, again, shows that wealth maximisation does not serve any human value as the cause of wealth maximisation would dictate that Amartya get the bowl of rice, and not Derek.

This example shows that wealth maximisation *per se* is not an appropriate goal for the law. Perhaps McBride is too quick to assume that Society 2 is necessarily inferior. For example, developing the above example: if in Society 2 Ronnie (and anyone in his position) donates their excess profits (here £9.50) to a charity fighting food poverty, we might argue that more good would have been done by the transaction than would occur in Society 1. But the point is that at least in our society it is not standard for the rich to give away profits to charity. Further, it would be the donation, rather than the sale, which was the beneficial transaction.

2.2.2 *Kantian Theories*

Under a Kantian approach private law provides each person a right to autonomy, with a corresponding duty to respect the autonomy of others. Under such an approach maximising autonomy is the law's primary goal. McBride (2019, p. 45) has challenged such an approach with this example:

> Suppose that I can save the lives of five people only by nudging you into a lever without your consent . . . Let's [call]. . . the society just before I nudge you into the lever 'Society 1' and the society after I nudge you into the lever (and save five people's lives) 'Society 2'. But this time we ask: 'Is Society 2 worse *in any respect* than Society 1?' It seems obvious that the answer is 'no' – there is no respect in which Society 2 is worse than Society 1, even though in Society 2 your independence has been violated in a way that it was not in Society 1. If this is right, then independence, of and in itself, is not of any value.

McBride's example shows that autonomy (or independence as he calls it) cannot be the sole value promoted by the law. Such an approach unjustifiably gives autonomy pre-eminence over many other values we hold dear (Foster 2009).

Placing autonomy at the heart of the response of the law is problematic for another reason. Holding people to a promise almost inevitably breaches their autonomy. It would mean that honouring the principle of autonomy was the justification for limiting autonomy. An obvious riposte might be that we are respecting an early autonomy (at the time of the promise) over current autonomy (at the time of the breach), but in many other areas of law current autonomy trumps past autonomy. Hence the consent of a patient to an operation last week cannot prevail over the refusal to consent on the day of the operation. Advance directives and other comparable declarations are an exception to the usual rule: they are effective only when the person will be unable to consent at the time in question. Hence the consent of the patient shortly before an operation to undergoing an anaesthetic will be legally effective when the patient is actually under the anaesthetic because, when under, no contradiction is possible.

2.2.3 *Public Good*

Some commentators see the primary role of private law as the promotion of peace and stability in the community. Goldberg and Zipursky (2020) are leading proponents of this view, and argue that private law is about providing victims of wrongdoing with civil recourse, without which people would seek to obtain their own compensation, perhaps by force, or would be left unremedied, either of which would challenge the stability of society. They explain:

> the common law of tort is particularly, perhaps uniquely, well-positioned to reinforce and clarify, but also to prompt and guide the revision of, norms of interaction that are crucial to the maintenance of civil society.

Other public goods from private law may be that contract law enables people to enter into beneficial transactions, and property law encourages people to undertake creative projects Hart (1994).

The difficulty with such claims being overriding goals of private law is that it is not difficult to think of uses of property rights that do not promote a good society (the preservation of obscene amounts of wealth by a few individuals, for instance) or similarly with contracts (for instance the corrupt awarding of public contracts by a Government to friends of the ruling party). We could imagine private law systems which seek to only promote the public good, but they would look very different from those that operate in common law jurisdictions.

2.2.4 Theories of Flourishing

McBride (2019) sees the primary role of the law as promoting flourishing, although that it is constrained by the extent to which the law needs to retain its legitimacy. He discusses this in two books (2019, 2020). In his first he sets out what theory he believes is currently underpinning the common law. He calls this RP—which stands both for 'reflective picture' and for 'received picture'—and it involves the participation in goods such as friendship, knowledge, aesthetic enjoyment, and play. The RP is *reflective* because it is 'the picture of human flourishing that most people living in modern Western liberal societies would endorse if they reflected for a while on what human flourishing involves'. The RP is also *received* because 'it is the picture of human flourishing that the culture of modern Western liberal societies encourages us to adopt when we consider what human flourishing involves'. Private law promotes this by

> (a) *protecting* them from suffering setbacks to their flourishing, and (b) *empowering* people to enter into transactions that will help them to flourish as human beings.

In his second book he promotes the understanding of flourishing which ought to underpin the private law. This focuses on leading a *truthful* life. He relies on the Journey Model of human flourishing which:

> assesses someone's flourishing according to what direction someone's life is going in. If it is heading in the 'right' direction, then that person is flourishing. If a person's life is heading in the 'wrong' direction, or going round in circles and not going in any direction at all, then that person is not flourishing as a human being.

He sees a flourishing life as one that is a journey towards G. G is something good "something that a human life ought to be directed at moving towards and achieving". That for McBride turns out to be truth. He explains:

> someone who lives in a truth-seeking community, engages in truth-seeking activities, and possesses the truth-seeking virtues is successfully engaged in a quest to lead a truthful life; and that if we can understand what these virtues and activities are, and what kind of community can claim to be a truth-seeking community, then we will understand what is involved in engaging in a quest to lead a truthful life and therefore... what it is to flourish as a human being.

It should be emphasised that McBride makes no claim as to what the truth is, and accepts it may be different for different people: it is the journeying towards it which is key.

This raises issues which are far too large for this book. It is notable that McBride thinks that much of private law, and certainly its practice, are inconsistent with his goal. He is certainly correct that litigation can encourage the use of tricks, lies and manipulation of facts which disguise the truth and hinder steps towards it. Whether, however, quotidian compliance with private law obligations does this is a matter of doubt.

2.2.5 *Legal Moralism*

These theories claim that private law is about "helping us do what we have reason – in fact, compelling reason – to do" (Gardner 2018, p. 4). It does this by adding legal obligations to the moral reasons to act, by requiring those who do not follow those reasons with an obligation to do what they can to repair the consequences of the breach, and by giving a choice to the victim to decide what remedy, if any, they may seek. Hence John Gardner (2018) argues that if D breaches a moral duty to C to do X, they will owe C a new duty to undo the harmful consequences that result from the breach of that duty. That, he suggests, is essentially what the remedies in contract law and tort law are doing.

One way of understanding the role of the law here is to see it as assisting individuals who face a wide range of competing moral claims on their time, energy and attention. Should I be writing a book; doing the laundry; visiting the lonely; or raising money for a charity? Private law offers help in navigating between the competing priorities by highlighting certain duties as of key importance. For example, if a person is facing competing calls on their resources, a contractual obligation is highlighted as to be undertaken before other, non-contractual undertakings. If there are competing calls on one's attention, the law of negligence highlights the need not to harm those around us. As Gardner (2018) put it: if there is a duty to act in a particular way then "some or all of the valid reasons not to do the required thing are to be discounted . ... A duty has some ability, in other words, to trump competing considerations."

Contract and (sometimes) tort law give us an opportunity to select duties: here we can see legal recognition of the importance of selecting goals one wants to achieve. Where one has committed to a particular project, one can be tempted off course by competing claims. The law can recognise that to adopt certain goals means that we take on a special commitment to them. For example, undertaking care of a child by a parent can mean that other calls on a parent's time or money need to be set aside. A book author commits to produce the manuscript by a certain time, and the contractual obligation can help to retain focus on that moral commitment. In effect, law authorises, and even requires, the parent to prioritise the claims of childcare over others they may face; and the author to focus on their manuscript deadline.

2.2.6 Putting the Theories Together

It would be surprising if a single theory were able to explain private law. We suggest that it can be helpful to combine a theory which explains the institution of private law and its impact on the community, and one which explains the obligations an individual has. The grander theories of human flourishing set out above work well at the level of explaining why we need something like a private law regime, but say little about why the individual should comply with the private law. The moralism arguments seem to do that job well. More simply, we might say that the private law helps an individual to do the right thing, and also promotes a society in which individuals can do good things.

Before moving on it is important to discuss two of the defining aspects of private law: the discretion of the victim whether to seek a remedy, and the use of law to resolve disputes.

The victim of a private wrong has a discretion to determine what remedy, if any, is pursued. While in the criminal law the state decides whether to bring the prosecution, in private law it is entirely a matter for the victim whether to bring proceedings. To John Gardner (2018) this is an important aspect of private law: it makes sure the law is not interfering in issues where it is not wanted. It encourages people to find non-court based solutions. Indeed, only a tiny percentage of potential legal claims are brought to court. While Gardner sees this as a strength of private law, to others it is potentially problematic. Anita Bernstein (2020) has argued that it may have gender implications. She sets out the extensive societal pressures on women which reward submission and punish "manifestations of aggression and self-regard". She notes that gendered poverty means women will have fewer financial resources to bring cases. She prefers an approach based on unjust enrichment which would not depend on a claim being brought by the "victim". Whether, given the extent of patriarchy, such an alternative approach will be any more effective as a remedy is open to debate. She highlights, however, a genuine tension in private law: we want parties to find imaginative ways of settling disputes, particularly if they avoid courts, but in doing so we may disadvantage women and other groups.

One of the key role of private law is then to resolve conflict. Where there is a dispute we need a reconciliation. Gardner (2018) suggests that reconciliation

> is one of the reasons why we have courts. Indeed, it is one of the reasons why we have law. But it is not true that conflict between people is in itself bad.

He goes on to note:

> The problem is not the conflict as such. There are some people with whom one has every reason to remain at odds. The problem is the escalation of the conflict into mean- spirited-ness, self- righteousness, pettiness, intolerance, bigotry, and so on. Such escalation, I would be the first to agree, should be avoided.

This analysis gives private law a particular role. First, private law offers guidance as to whether a wrong has been committed. Of course not all wrongs are recognised by the law of tort or contract: the unkind remark is not, for example. But where the wrong is a breach of private law, the fact of the legal breach provides the citizens involved with a clear indication that there is a serious wrong. It will often be the case that the parties will have their own way of righting that wrong. There may be an apology, a gift of a fresh pineapple, or a donation to a charity. But there are times when none of these informal means is effective. Then there needs to be something that seeks to restore the relationship. This is the second role of private law. It operates as a backstop: the final attempt to break the cycle of bitterness. In some cases that may be almost impossible. However, in many cases, some kind of moral restoration is required and achievable. The hurt and bitterness may continue, but the private law intervention has done what it can to put the relationship on a morally appropriate footing, right the wrong, restore an equilibrium between the parties, and give the parties room to move on.

To expand on that last point a little more, if we think about the nature of an apology we will note that at its heart is an acknowledgement that the person apologising wishes they had not acted as they had. "Fake apologies", beloved of some politicians, are fake precisely because they contain no such acknowledgment. "I am sorry my actions caused offence" is not the same as "I am sorry for my offensive actions". The latter clearly indicates that if the person were able to have their time again they would not have done the act. If should follow from this that a person apologising should do what they can to minimise the consequences of their act. This is what the remedies of the private law are seeking to do. That said, of course, private law is doomed to fail in some cases. Where the loss is emotional, or damage to the person, or, worse, loss of a loved one, nothing can be done to get close to the position before the wrongful act was done.

2.3 Contract Law

In light of the above we can see something of the role of contract law in making people good. It reinforces the message that people should keep their promises, and helps to create environments in which people can do good and flourish.

2.3.1 Promises and Contract Law

Nathan Oman (2012, p. 205) states "[M]ost judges, practitioners, and scholars accept that a contract consists of a legally enforceable promise." That is correct. But not all promises are legally enforced. The law selects certain kinds of promises as having a legal effect. Generally people accept that a promise carries an extra moral obligation, over and above a mere statement of intent (Wilkinson-Ryan 2020). Contracts go further in several ways. First, with a contract, the gravity of the promise is clearly indicated. The very existence of the contract is a sign that the issue is regarded as important by the parties and is intended to carry legal significance. Given the requirements for a legally valid contract, it should be hard for a party having entered a contract to turn around later and said, "I meant it as a joke" or "I did not mean you to take my comments as a proper promise". Second, contracts provide a mechanism for setting out in detail the arrangements between the parties. Generally a promise is made in vague terms, and is normally spoken. By entering a contract the parties are typically accepting that the substance of the agreement needs to be more explicit. Third, it is an acceptance by the parties that if a promise is not fulfilled some recompense might be expected. Of course, if you agree to meet a friend for coffee at 11 am no one expects that compensation could be due if you fail to make the date. That is a clear difference between a mere promise and a legally binding one.

To some commentators there is a difference between a promise and an agreement, and it is the agreement, rather than the promise, which is key. There are fine distinctions here. Suppose that X agrees to pay Y £50 to someone if Y mows X's lawn. Is that any different from *promising* to pay Y £50 for mowing the lawn. There are two senses in which it might be different. The first point is that, as contract lawyers know well, a mere promise, one for which there is no consideration (nothing given in exchange) is not binding. So in the above example a mere promise to pay £50 is not binding. This might indicate that it is not a promise per se which is key, but the *exchange* of promises. The difficulty with this view is that a bare promise, if expressed in terms of a deed, is binding, as are unilateral contracts, where the promisor forgoes the need to be informed of any agreement (e.g. where a reward is offered to a person who finds a lost dog). This suggests that the role of consideration is as evidence that the promise is to be taken seriously. The law's focus is on enforcing promises that are expressed and intended to be legally binding.

There is, however, a challenge if promises are to be seen as at the heart of contract law. If someone has promised to do something the *moral* obligation seems to be to carry that promise out. Yet the primary legal remedy in contract law is not specific performance but rather damages, intended to put the person in the position they would have been in had the contract been performed. If another person cân be found to do the same job at the same price at the same time then no damages at all will be awarded. However, we suggest this does not necessarily indicate that promises are not the basis of contract law.

Usually contracts are fulfilled. Contract law by and large succeeds in its objective of making contracts enforceable. If contracts are broken, in practice refunds are normally offered, apologetic gift cards are sent, and people move on. The cases that come to court are the exceptional ones. They are the cases when the norms of apology, flexibility and making alternative arrangements have broken down. It is in this light that the legal response to the breakdown should be viewed. As the relationship between the parties has broken down, it is not necessarily desirable to compel performance of the contract. You may not want your courtroom adversary doing work in your house, for example. Damages, enabling you to find an alternative contractor, may be far preferable. You can establish a new contractual relationship, rather than being forced to retain an unwanted relationship.

Charles Fried (1981) uses a helpful example of a music lover who buys the flat next door to a violinist who regularly convenes a strong quartet. The violinist may know that the music lover has bought the apartment specifically to enjoy the music, but this imposes no obligation on the violinist to continue convening the quartet, and no inhibition on him deciding to meet at the cellist's house instead. The music lover bought the flat, relying on the presumption that the violinist would continue to convene the quartet, but that alone is insufficient to require the violinist to continue to play music. Fried (2014) claims that contract law provides a

> structure by which actors could determine for themselves the terms of their interaction and cooperation— whether in commercial or personal relations... .Promise is a kind of moral invention: its mode of causation is moral causation; it allows persons to create obligation where there was none before, and thus it gives free individuals a facility for extending their reach by enlisting the reliable collaboration of other free persons.

So: had the music lover wanted to bind the violinist to convening the quartet they would have needed to enter into a contract. The violinist would have needed to decide whether they wished to prioritize performing for their neighbour (say on Monday nights) over other claims. We might expect that the violinist would not want to assume such an obligation, recognising that their obligation to the fellow members of the quartet might require them to meet at another venue, or that other Monday-night obligations might mean there could be no rehearsal. Indeed it is highly unlikely the violinist would agree to such an undertaking unless they were receiving a valuable undertaking in return (e.g. that the music lover would pay money each week). If the music lover wanted to guarantee string quartet music every Monday night, a formal, legally binding contract would be necessary. An assurance that 'so long as it is not inconvenient we will play every Monday' would not be sufficient. The music lover needs a promise that will be honoured, however inconvenient it is to do so. And if the violinist agrees to play every Monday night in return for payment, the violinist will not be satisfied with a promise to pay 'so long as it is not inconvenient'. Contract provides a mechanism for the kind of promises they need.

2.3.2 Good Faith and Contract Law

We have seen that contracts provide a structure within which personally and socially helpful activities can take place. However, of course, contract law has a dark side. Unregulated contract law gives a stronger party ample opportunity to exploit a weaker party (Brooks 2020). Indeed, contract law may give legal support to conduct which is not good: it may, for instance, enforce payment of an agreement to provide anti-personnel mines designed to kill civilians. A (very) few contracts are void on grounds on public policy (an attempt to address the type of mischief illustrated by the anti-personnel mines example), and in an attempt to address the issue of inequality of bargaining position most legal systems have a concept of good faith and the principle that duress might vitiate a contract. While many contracts are entered into to make an economic gain, contracts which are solely to the benefit of one party will be harmful. We would put this in a positive way: contracting parties owe each other a duty to deal fairly with each other. Daniel Markovits (2014) has argued that the duty of good faith is "contract's core value....Good faith thus constitutes contracts as ... collaborations."

In legal doctrine the regulation of contracts, to achieve good faith, broadly falls into three categories. First, there are those rules governing the creation of the contract: requiring parties not to engage in fraud, misrepresentation, taking advantage of mistakes and the like. In other words the focus is on the fairness of the negotiations leading to the contract. Second, there are doctrines which will strike down the substance of terms which are unfair. Third, there are doctrines dealing with enforceability and the circumstances in which it may be unfair to enforce a contract—such as the doctrine of frustration. These categories overlap.

Some jurisdictions impose a general duty of good faith. For example in the United States the *Restatement (Second) of Contracts* 1981 § 205 cmt. states that "[e] very contract imposes upon each party a duty of good faith and fair dealing in its performance and its enforcement." In English law there is no such general duty, although the principle behind that duty can be seen in a range of English doctrines. In English law, however, the relevant doctrines focus mainly on good faith in the bargaining process, rather than on the substance of the contract. John Cartwright (1991, p. 213), expressing the traditional English approach, explains:

> Parties are free to bargain; and to bargain well or badly. But if one, party, by his words or conduct, or by abusing a position of strength which he held vis a vis the other party, disturbs the balance of the negotiations, the disadvantaged party should have appropriate remedy..... [Otherwise] contacts should be upheld, and parties should not be able to extricate themselves from contracts just because they have not obtained the benefit for which they hoped.

This is not the place to explore in detail how a duty of good faith might be understood, but we emphasise three points.

First, in English law the extent to which good faith is required can vary between cases. Transactions between two businesses may be very different from cases where a business contracts directly with a consumer—and accordingly consumers are given particular legal protection. This demonstrates an awareness of the inherent inequality of bargaining power and resources between consumers and businesses.

Second, the law places particular emphasis on non-key terms. Those are terms which do not define the item or the price, but, for example, deal with excluding liability or permitting variation of the contract. The thinking here is that it is unlikely a consumer will be unaware of what they are buying or the price, but they may well be unaware of complex exclusion clauses.

We believe that there is a good case for good faith requirements in all contracts, recognising that what might be required of good faith may vary depending on the identity of the parties. First, we suggest it reflects the nature of a contract, which should be a *cooperation*. It recognises that not everything can be put into a contract, and where a contract cannot make explicit provision for something that subsequently proves important, an assumption of good faith might fill the gap.

Second, and to similar effect, we can see a requirement of good faith as an implied term of a contract. Leggatt J took this approach in *Yam Seng Pie Ltd. v International Trade Corp Ltd.* [2013] EWHC 111 (QB)). He argued that we could take it that two parties entering a contract would be agreeing to act in good faith towards each other. They could be seen as the "shared values and norms of behaviour" that citizens in contracts expect from each other, including the "core value of honesty". By contrast Lord Ackner in *Walford and others v Miles and another* [1992] 2 AC 128 (HL) stated:

> [T]he concept of a duty to carry on negotiations in good faith is inherently repugnant to the adversarial position of the parties when involved in negotiations. Each party to the negotiations is entitled to pursue his (or her) own interest, so long as he avoids making misrepresentations. ... A duty to negotiate in good faith is as unworkable in practice as it is inherently inconsistent with the position of a negotiating party.

Relying on the implied term approach, the truth may be that there is no consensus among the business community on issues of good faith, but if so, the law needs to determine the ruling norms. The norm should be that contracting parties act in good faith. As Roger Brownsword (2000) argues:

> the whole purpose of good faith is to bring contract doctrine into line with the standards of fair dealing that are accepted in particular business communities. Whilst the standards of some business communities might be ruthlessly competitive, allowing for non-disclosure, opportunistic termination, shirking and so on, in other communities such practices might be regarded as unfair.

Arguments over good faith reflect the norm of the self which is used by the law. Traditional contract law is essentially neoliberal—premised on the ideal of the self-sufficient, informed, autonomous businessman who should be free to make his business deals for himself. Individual liberty is protected: any truncation of that liberty by legislators is deprecated. It is not for the courts or the government to interfere in contractual freedom by seeking to declare that the terms of a particular contract are unfair or inappropriate for the parties. This is closely tied to the principle of autonomy: as long as a person has capacity, their choices should be respected.

That includes respecting the choices of a person who decides to bind themselves under a contract.

However, in contracts there are two parties. An approach which protects freedom of contract will favour the stronger contractor. Contracting parties are assumed to be knowledgeable, able to stand up for themselves, and, absent improper behaviour, on an equal footing to bargain for themselves. The values that are promoted by contract law are those of self-interest, the promotion of free-markets, self-sufficiency, and profit maximization. But the law sometimes—and particularly in the consumer context, allows contracts to reflect the power, or the lack of power, of the parties. It generally does so by reference to the norm of the (notional) average consumer who is seen as 'reasonably well informed, observant and circumspect'.

As we have argued previously (Foster and Herring 2017) a more accurate understanding of human nature than that embodied in the philosophy of the free-market, is to acknowledge that we are all vulnerable. A better norm than the neoliberal norm would be to arrange contract law on the assumption that contracting parties are ignorant of many things, are open to emotional and physical pressures, and who do not have the time, energy, or legal ability to read and understand mountains of paperwork. We should approach our contracting partners as those with whom we want to have a fair relationship—as people who are more than a source of profit; as vulnerable fellow travellers for whom we should look out.

Such a vision of contract law would expect and require the parties to take reasonable steps to ensure that the other party is aware of the important terms of the contract, and not mistaken about any significant part of it. The law would seek to ensure that the terms of the contract were in line with a fair balancing of rights and responsibilities. The law would be alert to the misuse of relationships to obtain an advantage for one party over another. We could have such a contract law, although we are currently far from it.

2.3.3 Distinguishing Contracts and Torts

Tort has its own chapter in this book (Chap. 3), but we highlight here two key differences between a contract and a tort claim. First, a contractual duty is chosen, whereas many tort law duties are imposed whether we like it or not. The distinction is not watertight: tort law duties can sometimes be modified or excluded by notices or by assuming special duties of care, but most tortious duties are imposed by simple operation of the law. These differences between contract and tort indicate the different moral virtues in play. We owe all those we come across a duty to take care of a basic kind, as we shall see later. However, the duties imposed by the law can be in conflict with one another, and if the law creates competition between different duties, it needs to prescribe methods for the resolution of the competing claims. The law of tort, as we will see, does this by reference to the concept of reasonableness. However, a contractual promise is an undertaking to prioritise a certain obligation among all others. People are only willing to enter into a contract on the understanding that the other party will so prioritise the obligation. Hence while the primary response of tort law remedies is to seek to undo the consequences of the wrong, remedies for breach of contract seek to put the parties in the position in which they would have been had the contractual promise been fulfilled.

A second important distinction is that the tort law duty depends on reasonableness. A contractual breach can arise even if the promisor has taken all reasonable steps to avoid the breach. Contractual breach is a matter of strict liability. Joseph Raz (2014) contrasts remedies under tort and contract law. Tort law obligations depend on the nature of the action and its context. So you could not know from the mere fact that Jonathan knocked Charles over that a tort law beach had occurred. We would need to know if there were ways Jonathan could have avoided the collision; whether there were good reason for knocking Charles over (was he about to be hit by a bicycle) etc.? However in in relation to promises this is different. As Raz (2014) explains:

> If I promise to feed your cat next week, to come to your party, to send flowers in your name to your mother on Mother's Day, to lend you my new DVD, or whatever the action I promise to perform (or to refrain from) the reason is the same: my promise.

The nature of the act or its circumstances are irrelevant: it is the breach of the promise which is wrong and gives the right to a remedy.

While contract represents a special undertaking to another, at the heart of tort law is the duty to take care not to harm all those one encounters. We will illustrate this by reference to the tort of negligence, although other torts could be used. In *Donoghue v Stevenson* [1932] UKHL 100, Lord Atkin wrote:

> You must take reasonable care to avoid acts or omissions which you can reasonably foresee would be likely to injure your neighbour. Who, then, in law, is my neighbour? The answer seems to be— persons who are so closely and directly affected by my act that I ought reasonably to have them in contemplation as being so affected when I am directing my mind to the acts or omissions which are called in question.

Thus the reasonable person is a core concept in negligence. Heidi Li Feldman (2000) notes that:

> [t]ort law assesses negligence according to the conduct of a reasonable person of ordinary prudence who acts with due care for the safety of others ....It is mistaken to reduce negligence to reasonableness or to try to understand the sense of reasonableness contemplated by the negligence standard without reference to the virtues of prudence and benevolence.

On this approach the reasonable person test includes the duty to take care that one does not injure others (prudence) and to care for others (benevolence). In this way the law of tort informs citizens what conduct will generate a liability to compensate a victim and, more importantly, what they need to do to avoid being subject to that liability. In short it compares the conduct of the citizen with to the normative ethically well-motivated person who takes care not to injure others and acts reasonably.

The significance of *Donoghue v Stevenson* is that duties under tort law are not restricted to family member or employees, but are owed to everyone. It acknowledges that when it comes to (at least) death or physical injury the interests of all we come across should count. We should not ignore the life or wellbeing of another just because they are not in our club, group or family. We can, if we wish, take on extra obligations to reflect particular projects, but that will be done generally through contract, or by explicitly adopting a particular and unusual duty of care in the law of tort (such as when a doctor in a publicly funded health system, who has no contractual duty to a patient, and no duty from anywhere in the law to take on a particular patient, nonetheless decides to enter into a doctor-patient relationship with a patient, which will result in the creation of a special set of obligations in the law of tort).

2.4 Property

The concept of property is complex. A popular understanding is that it should be seen as a bundle of rights. James Penner (2020, p. 279) explains it like this:

> Any legal configuration understood to be a property right, say a fee simple in Blackacre, is in fact an aggregate of norms, such as the liberty to enter Blackacre, the power to license others to enter, the liberty to build upon Blackacre, the power to grant an easement over Blackacre, and so on. There is no necessary and sufficient set of these constituting norms which make up the "property right" to Blackacre. Different aggregates will occur in different circumstances, and so the legal labelling of some such aggregate as a "property" right cannot properly be done on the basis of some central constituting norms, such as the right that others exclude themselves from Blackacre, or the right to deal with the title to Blackacre.

At one level we may justify the institution of property as simply a set of rules which avoid people having disputes over things. Hence John Stuart Mill (1848) saw the primary function of private property as the preservation of peace. But that does not really explain what kind of property regime is appropriate. We still need some account of why it is that X, rather than Y, is given control rights over a piece of property. Indeed if there is not seen to be a degree of fairness in the allocation it will not succeed in its aim of preserving peace.

One highly influential theory has been John Locke's account, which emphasised the argument that the investment of labour justified a claim of ownership. The person who had planted and tendered the seeds had thereby a claim to own the resulting vegetables. Daniel Attas (2007) puts it this way:

> The reason is that by incorporating it in a project, or investing it with one's personhood, *X* is made necessary for the promotion of values such as need, welfare or the realization of self-consciousness *for P*. Spheres of control are determined by individuals taking possession of unowned parts of the world, by occupying, laboring, using or placing their will in objects, thereby gaining entitlements to control the object and to the income it generates to the necessary extent.

There is clearly much that is attractive about this view. It seems to acknowledge an intuition that hard work should not go unrewarded, and that as compared with anyone else the person who has invested the time and effort on an item has a stronger claim to it. Or, putting it another way, that a person who seeks to claim an item which another has created, without compensating that other for it, is being unjustly enriched. As Jim Harris (1996, p. 365) suggests, it may be that labour needs to be listed alongside the more conventionally considered criteria in order to provide a full justification for the institution of property:

> In the end, we are left with a mix of property-specific justice reasons – property freedoms, labour-desert, privacy, incentives and markets, independence and basic needs. None of these imports precise, context-free considerations and their mix and do no more than structure our answers to general or specific problems. . . . .[P]roperty questions are inseparably affected by the social setting in which a property institution exists.

As this quote indicates, much depends on the society within which the property regime exists. For example, Locke's approach seems to assume that all are equally able to provide labour. Harris' formulation also does not clearly differentiate what kinds of labour are to count. David Lametti (2020) writes

> By definition, private property involve the distribution of resources and allocation of powers of control and use to a privileged person. It distribution will necessarily exclude others to some extent. It distribution will also confer social and political power to some over others, all of which has an ongoing distributional impact. It also confers a great deal of autonomy to the individual.

One particular concern is that many forms of labour go unacknowledged in our society. An important example is the labour of care work, which is largely unvalued or acknowledged in the law (Herring 2013). In part this is because the product of care (human wellbeing) is not assessed in a way that can be measured in a monetary way—and anything that does not have a visible economic value is often assumed to have no value at all. Another reason is that care is primarily performed by women, and in a patriarchal society men determine what counts as work, value and production. Many other examples of how the property regime privileges certain forms of labour over others could be given. However, these do not go the heart of whether property law could, in an ideal society, promote good. These points are criticisms of what counts as labour, rather the basis of the labour principle itself.

A major challenge to property is its treatment of the "commons". Stephen Munzer (2005) explains

> a commons is a resource which all have a liberty-right to use, from which no one has a normative power to exclude others, and which no one has a duty to refrain from exploiting.

In other words a commons is a public good, to which all should have access. An example might be a mountain designated as a national park, a village green, the oceans, or fresh air. Any member of the community should be able to access the resource, but unless the whole community agrees none should be denied it. There are clearly great benefits to society in creating and preserving these public goods. They, however, do not fit within traditional images of property which are about excluding and controlling. If left outside the property paradigm there is the danger of "the tragedy of the commons." This arises because if all the members of the community use the resource sensibly it can benefit all considerably. However, the freedom of access can mean that a selfishly-minded person can overuse the resource for their own good, and deprive others of it. Imagine, for example, a village common. Each villager lets their animals roam on it, and there is just about enough grass for all. However, each villager could rationally consider whether it would be worth them adding an animal to their herd. They might calculate that doing so would increase their income at little cost, as the common land can feed the additional sheep. It might be that the extra animal will mean there is slightly less grass for all the animals and that might very slightly affect the villagers income, but by far less than the income of the extra animal. However, if all the villagers do a similar calculation and accordingly get extra animals, there will be overgrazing and in due course the land will become useless. And there is the tragedy. If the ruling criterion is simply individual enrichment, the resource upon which they all depend will be destroyed.

The problem is that property models, at least as understood in common law jurisdictions, are largely based on individualistic values that protect rights of exclusion and control.

Property rights protect one particular set of interests: the interests of control, exclusion and transfer. Larissa Katz (2008) has captured the nature of property interests well. She writes:

> First, familiar property law doctrines . . . carve out a position of authority for owners that is neither derived from nor subordinate to any other's. These and other rules create the institutional structure that permits the owner to function as the supreme agenda setter for the resource.

This favouring of the interests of the individual, and allowing the owner to "set the agenda" is at the heart of property rights. This means that communal assets do not fit into the regime. Nor indeed assets that an individual might own, but in which the community has a legitimate interest.

To conclude, we do need some form of property regulation to determine ownership. The problem is that the law reflects some of the flaws in our society in failing to recognise the value of some forms of labour, such as care work, and overvaluing individual interests while neglecting important communal values.

2.5 Conclusion

There is much in private law that provides a framework so that people can be good. In our society people do generally keep their promises, respect people's property, and take care not to injure people. Where this is not done there are many informal ways of apologising and making amends. The courts, where they do intervene, offer some guidance on how these informal arrangements should work: people should seek to keep their promises or ensure the other party has not lost out as a result: where someone has been injured through carelessness they should receive compensation.

We have, however, also highlighted areas where private law could do more to encourage good behaviour. Embodying a duty of good faith in contract law, acknowledging the value of care in property law, and finding ways in property law to protect communal interests would lead to more ethically justifiable laws.

References

Attas D (2007) Fragmenting property. Law Philosophy 25(1):119–149

Bernstein A (2020) A feminist perspective: private law as unjust enrichment. In: Gold A, Goldberg J, Kelly D, Sherwin E, Smith H (eds) The Oxford handbook of the new private law. Oxford University Press, Oxford

Brooks R (2020) Good faith in contractual exchanges. In: Gold A, Goldberg J, Kelly D, Sherwin E, Smith H (eds) The Oxford handbook of the new private law. Oxford University Press, Oxford

Brownsword R (2000) Review, Angelo Forte (ed) Good faith in contract and property law. Mod Law Rev 58:940–942

Cartwright J (1991) Unequal bargaining. Clarendon Press, Oxford

Feldman H (2000) Prudence, benevolence and negligence: virtue ethics and tort law. Chicago-Kent Law Rev 74:1431–1466

Foster C (2009) Choosing life, choosing death: the tyranny of autonomy in medical ethics and law. Hart, Oxford

Foster C, Herring J (2017) Identity, personhood and the law. Springer, Chan

Fried C (1981) Contract as promise. Oxford University Press, Oxford

Fried C (2014) The ambition of contract as promise. In: Klass G, Letsas G, Sapria P (eds) Philosophical foundations of contract law. Oxford University Press, Oxford

Gardner J (2018) From personal life to private law. Oxford University Press, Oxford

Goldberg J, Zipursky B (2020) Recognizing wrongs. Belknap Press, New York

Harris JW (1996) Property and justice. Oxford University Press, Oxford

Hart HLA (1994) The concept of law. Oxford University Press, Oxford

Herring J (2013) Caring and the law. Hart, Oxford

Katz L (2008) Exclusion and exclusivity in property law. Univ Toronto Law J 58:275–304

Lametti D (2020) The (virtue) ethics of private property. In: Gold A, Goldberg J, Kelly D, Sherwin E, Smith H (eds) The Oxford handbook of the new private law. Oxford University Press, Oxford

Markovits D (2014) Good Faith as contract's core value. In: Klass G, Letsas G, Sapria P (eds) Philosophical foundations of contract law. Oxford University Press, Oxford

McBride N (2019) The humanity of private law: part I. Hart, Oxford

McBride N (2020) The humanity of private law: part II. Hart, Oxford

Mill JS (1848) Principles of political economy. John W. Parker, West Strand, London

Munzer S (2005) The commons and the anticommons in the law and theory of property. In: Golding G, Edmundson W (eds) The Blackwell guide to philosophy of law and legal theory. Blackwell, London

Oman N (2012) Markets as a moral foundation for contract law. Iowa Law Rev 98:183–215

Penner J (2020) Property. In: Gold A, Goldberg J, Kelly D, Sherwin E, Smith H (eds) The Oxford handbook of the new private law. Oxford University Press, Oxford

Posner E (2001) Contract law and theory. Aspen Publishers, Aspen CO

Raz J (2014) Is there a reason to keep a promise? In: Klass G, Letsas G, Sapria P (eds) Philosophical foundations of contract law. Oxford University Press, Oxford

Wilkinson-Ryan T (2020) Psychology and the new private law. In: Gold A, Goldberg J, Kelly D, Sherwin E, Smith H (eds) The Oxford handbook of the new private law. Oxford University Press, Oxford

Chapter 3
Tort

Abstract This chapter argues there is only a limited role for the law of tort in the promotion of personal morality. The circumstances in which tort law imposes duties are limited, and the law is generally uninterested in whether the tortfeasor has a blameworthy state of mind. The other rules of tort law, especially the law of causation, diminish any role the law of tort may otherwise have in promoting morality.

Keywords Negligence · Tort · Duty of care · Public law · Private law

3.1 Introduction

Many English lawyers instinctively think that the law of tort has nothing to do with private (or indeed public) morality. This is the consequence of a number of assumptions.

First, it is assumed that law is divided neatly into public and private law. Second, that tort is very definitely part of private law. Third, that morality, insofar as it is the business of the law at all, is the business of public law. And fourth, that the primary business of tort is mere compensation—putting the claimant back into the position she would have been in had the tort not occurred, being careful neither to undercompensate nor overcompensate.

In this chapter we interrogate each of these assumptions, concluding that each is an oversimplification, and that tort can indeed be an effective agent of individual morality, as indeed it has been in the past.

3.2 A Historical Overview

The distinction between crime and tort is a relatively recent one. Even now, as we will see, the boundary between the two domains is far from clear. In antiquity it was even fuzzier.

© The Author(s), under exclusive license to Springer Nature Switzerland AG 2021
C. Foster, J. Herring, *The Law as a Moral Agent*, SpringerBriefs in Law,
https://doi.org/10.1007/978-3-030-71334-8_3

In the ancient Mesopotamian Code of Hammurabi, dated to around 1754 BC, the distinction between penalty and restitution is constantly blurred. Take, for instance, the Code's version of the rule in *Rylands v Fletcher:*

> If anyone be too apathetic to keep his dam in primly condition, and does not so keep it; if then the dam break and all the fields be flooded, then shall he in whose dam the break occurred be sold for money, and the money shall replace the crops which he has caused to be ruined. (Law 53)

This has a distinctly modern tortious feel to it—apart from the jarring note about selling the tortfeasor. But that note is important. What if the tortfeasor's funds were sufficient to make full monetary restitution? It did not matter: the penalty was part of the package. One might say that the Code was more holistically concerned with restitution than modern remedies: that it recognised that money isn't everything, and that (as today's practitioners acknowledge), the motive for litigation is often, inter alia, vengeance.

We see the same in the best-known clause of the Code—a clause whose words, if not spirit, found its way into the famous Biblical ordinances (Leviticus 24: 19–20; Exodus 21:24; Deuteronomy 19:21): 'If a man destroy the eye of another man' (says the Code of Hammurabi, Law 196), 'they shall destroy his eye. If one break a man's bone, they shall break his bone. If one destroy the eye of a freeman or break the bone of a freeman he shall pay one gold mina. If one destroy the eye of a man's slave or break a bone of a man's slave he shall pay one-half his price.' Sometimes money will be enough: sometimes not.

Law 53 (about the breakage of dams) is unusual in specifying the mental element ('apathetic') associated with liability. Like most Codes that followed—and like the modern law of tort (which, generally but not always, requires proof of loss or damage)—the Code's main concern is with the consequences of an act or omission.

The Code is striking for the values it exhibits. Generally, property is more important than human life or physical integrity. Robbers, for instance, are put to death (Law 22).

In the hands of the Hebrews, the Code's rules were mitigated and nuanced. 'An eye for an eye' was taken to mean *only* one eye. The emphasis on property rather than the person was softened or reversed. But the frontier between compensation and penalty remained uncertain or non-existent.

The paradigm case of a civil law system was that of ancient Rome, yet it had distinctly penal elements too. In relation to the early common law, Matthew Dyson (2014) observes that '. . .crime' and 'tort' as we call them now, were equally valid ways for a victim to pursue justice for a wrongful act. The choice seems to have been between *compensation* and *vengeance,* and this choice was one for the victim.' He notes that it is unclear when the need for a distinction between the two domains was recognised, but cites Lord Mansfield, who, in *Atcheson v Everitt* (1775) 98 ER 1142, 1147, perhaps rather overstating the case, said that '[T]here is no distinction better known, than the distinction between civil and criminal law.' If the distinction was real, its effect was far from obvious. Civil and criminal law continued to share and exchange territory in England and elsewhere. Mediaeval Swedish law distinguished not between crime and tort, but between wrongs to society and wrongs to individuals—a sophisticated and prescient distinction which may be thought to have anticipated by half a millennium the modern jurisprudence of the European Convention on Human Rights, a corpus of law to which we will return. French law, too, was late in distinguishing between crime and civil law (Dyson 2014).

The law of tort—perhaps more than any other area of law, with the arguable exception of crime—has always reflected society's view of itself and its view of the status of the individual. It has tended to follow, rather than form, that view. At least until human rights started to be grafted into its body, it has tended to be conservative and descriptive rather than aspirational. Deakin and Adams (2019, p. 6), commenting on the late recognition of civil liability for psychiatric harm, observe that 'When English tort law was formed, it was shaped to meet the needs of a society emerging from feudalism....' and accordingly psychiatric harm 'could receive no attention in a world accustomed to extreme physical suffering.' This is a good illustration of the general principle: tort law reacts to and embodies norms created elsewhere: it does not, by and large, create new norms or shape old ones.

It is therefore unsurprising that the expressed or implied aims of the law of tort have fluctuated. Deakin and Adams (2019, p. 43) note that they have included 'appeasement, justice, punishment, deterrence, compensation, and loss-spreading' and that none of these aims has at any time 'offered a complete justification for the law...' In this chapter we examine each of the aims identified by Deakin and Adams, asking how, if at all, each is connected to the promotion of individual morality.

3.3 Tort: Private or Public Law?

Most modern lawyers, at least in the west, would regard criminal law as a province of public law: its primary function is to enforce rules that have been formulated by the state, and enforcement is by state agencies (such as the police and the prison service). Judges too are paid by the state. In England they sit under the Royal Crest, dispensing the Queen's justice. There is an important separation of powers, whereby the judiciary is in many ways independent of the executive and the legislature (both of whose acts and omissions the judges may have to censure), but at root the judges are part of the state's machinery for ensuring that the state's rules are kept; that public morality is vindicated. Since there will be at least some overlap between public and private morality, modern criminal law is clearly an agent of private morality, even if its private functions are carried out primarily in the name of the public.

Is the law of tort really so different? The modern law of tort is mainly concerned with the regulation of certain specified relationships between some individuals. The individuals concerned are not always individual human beings: they may be corporate bodies of various kinds. They may, indeed, be organs of the state—for instance government departments. Where the defendant in a tort claim is a branch of the state, and (at least) where the claim might be said to have some sort of moral colour, it is hard to resist the observation that the law of tort has a public law function.

The fact that tort claims are adjudicated by state-funded judges, applying law that is the law of the land and which embodies to some extent societal views about how humans should behave to one another, again gives some public law character to the law of tort. One of the frequently cited reasons for the importance of making good laws is that laws express the values of a society, and that the mere expression of those values itself tends to affect behaviour. We examine this contention specifically in the context of tort law's view of *fault,* but simply observe for the moment that *any* expressivist function of the law might be thought to be a quintessentially public law function.

Ultimately we are not convinced that the much vaunted distinction between public and private law is real at all, or, if it is, that it does a great deal of useful work. There is one important exception: sometimes objectives that are ethically illegitimate in the context of a tort law dispute (precisely because of its residual private law character) will be positively ethically desirable if translated into an unequivocally public law context (such as criminal law). We discuss this below.

We agree with Duff (2014) that there is no very obvious set of criteria with which to determine whether a particular wrong should be regarded as criminal and which tortious. What is clearer, though, is whether a criminal or tortious system is best suited for the legal handling of various wrongs, but clarity about this demands a close examination of the functions of tort and crime with a view to evaluating their objectives and the efficacy with which they discharge those objectives. We now embark on that examination for the law of tort.

3.4 Tort as Appeasement, Justice, Punishment, and Deterrence

Feuds resulting from actual or perceived wrongs are important, and sometimes defining, elements of many societies. They are emotionally and financially costly, not only to those immediately involved, but also to society more broadly. A continually feuding society is one in which the rule of law does not reign. To transfer private feuds into the judicial space reduces both their wider societal fall-out and the potential for physical, financial and moral overreaction.

Some may say, though, that the need to be appeased by causing the suffering (whether physical, financial, or otherwise) of another is itself morally illegitimate, and that a morally well-oriented society should frown on that desire and refuse to accommodate and systematize it within its adjudicatory structure.

We disagree. The desire for appeasement is an element of the desire for justice, and the need to 'make the offender pay' is so deeply ingrained in the human psyche that it cannot be legislated away. Far from being an immoral impulse, it is an expression of one of the most fundamental moral instincts. We note that while rehabilitation and reparation have recently, at least in the west, become more prominent as sentencing objectives than punishment, the punitive element is recognised to be a crucial part of the justification for many criminal sentences.

Our disagreement with appeasement, justice, and punishment as justifications for the law of tort are not primarily moral, but practical. We contend below that tort should be primarily concerned with compensation, and a tort system that compensates effectively will necessarily not be a good vehicle for appeasement, justice, or punishment. There are several reasons for this.

First: the means of compensation is and should be primarily monetary. This is the case now in most western systems. There are other remedies (notably injunctions of various kinds), but non-monetary relief (as opposed to an order for specific performance in the law of contract) is relatively unimportant in the law of tort, except as interlocutory relief.

Yet monetary damages are not *emotionally* satisfactory for many of the types of loss and damage encountered in the law of tort. The classic example is damages for pain, suffering, and loss of amenity. Claimants commonly and understandably complain that these damages are derisory and insulting. They do not seem *fair,* and so do not satisfy the emotional demands of justice. Money cannot adequately compensate for pain and suffering: one is not comparing like with like. Yet to compensate like with like is unthinkable except in the criminal (and therefore unambiguously public law context), in which the state causes pain (by way of imprisonment, for instance) to match the pain of a victim.

Second: in many cases the damages will not be paid by the tortfeasor, but by an insurer. A claimant who seeks retribution will not be satisfied if the only real consequence for the tortfeasor will be the loss of a no-claims bonus or a small uplift in the insurance premium they subsequently have to pay. It seems perverse to un-wish or make unlawful the whole insurance industry in order to make the payment of damages a real punishment. It would be particularly perverse where, as often, there is real disproportion between the (small) magnitude of the tortfeasor's fault (if any) and the (huge) damages payable.

Third: an efficient compensatory system will seek to avoid trials, and will aim to resolve disputes quickly, cheaply, and in a way that avoids confrontation between the claimant and the defendant. Yet confrontation is often precisely what that the claimant wants. She often wants to see the defendant sweating under cross-examination: that is a part of the punitive objective.

Fourth: a related point is that the claimant will often want, too, a detailed inquiry into the facts of the situation that ground the claim. That inquiry will be seen as part of the business of justice: of ensuring that nothing is swept under the carpet. Yet many of the facts seen as important by the claimant will have no part in the limited inquiry necessary to ensure that the elements necessary to establish liability are made out, and the scientifically calculated sum of damages due is properly assessed.

There are a few modern instances of punishment being the express purpose of an order made in a tort claim. Punitive/exemplary damages are occasionally awarded in

England. Scotland, Australia, Canada, and New Zealand have declined to follow the English example.[1]

The key English case on punitive damages is *Rookes v Barnard (No. 1)*. It needs to be considered alongside the subsequent House of Lords case of *Cassell v Broome* [1972] AC 1027, in which Lord Hailsham cautioned against seeing *Rookes* as a complete rationalisation of the law of exemplary damages. (at 1076) In *Rookes* Lord Devlin embarked on a comprehensive review of the authorities, concluding that 'your Lordships could not without a complete disregard of precedent, and indeed of statute, now arrive at a determination that refused altogether to recognise the exemplary principle.' (at 1226) He went on to describe the purpose of such damages: '. . .there are certain categories of cases in which an award of exemplary damages can serve a useful purpose in vindicating the strength of the law and thus affording a practical justification for admitting into the civil law a principle which ought logically to belong to the criminal.' (at 1226)

The two categories in which such damages can be properly awarded are, first, 'oppressive, arbitrary or unconstitutional action by the servants of the government.' (at 1226) Lord Devlin was careful to say that this should not extend to oppressive action by private corporations or individuals: 'Where one man is more powerful than another, it is inevitable that he will try to use his power to gain his ends; and if his power is much greater than the other's, he might perhaps be said to be using it oppressively. If he uses his power illegally, he must of course pay for his illegality in the ordinary way; but he is not to be punished simply because he is the more powerful. In the case of the government it is different, for the servants of the government are also the servants of the people and the use of their power must always be subordinate to their duty of service. It is true that there is something repugnant about a big man bullying a small man and very likely the bullying will be a source of humiliation that makes the case one for aggravated damages, but it is not in my opinion punishable by damages.' (at 1226)

In *Cassell* Lord Reid (who had agreed with Lord Devlin in *Rookes*) clarified that this category was never intended to be limited to Crown servants. 'The [material] contrast is between "the government" and private individuals. Local government is as much government as national government, and the police and many other persons are exercising governmental functions. It was unnecessary in *Rookes v. Barnard* to define the exact limits of the category. I should certainly read it as extending to all those who by common law or statute are exercising functions of a governmental character.' (at 1008)[2]

---

[1]Note, for instance, Lord Hailsham's observation in *Cassell v Broome No. 1* [1972] UKHL [1972] AC 1027 at 1052–1053, where he noted the 'somewhat cool reception in the Commonwealth of *Rookes* v. *Barnard*, particularly in the Australian Supreme Court decision in *Uren* v. *John Fairfax and Sons Pty. Ltd.* [1967] A.L.R. 25 which had been affirmed so far as regards Australian law by the Judicial Committee of the Privy Council in the associated case of *Australian Consolidated Press Ltd.* v. *Uren* [1969] 1 A.C. 590.'

[2]Note too Lord Hailsham's observation, at 1077–1078: 'I would be surprised if it included only servants of the Government in the strict sense of the word. It would, in my view, obviously apply to

Lord Devlin's second category is those 'in which the Defendant's conduct has been calculated by him to make a profit for himself which may well exceed the compensation payable to the plaintiff.' (at 1227) This was, he noted, a factor conventionally taken into account in assessing damages for defamation: a defendant 'should not be allowed to sell another man's reputation for profit.' (at 1227) He continued: Where a Defendant with a cynical disregard for a [claimant's] rights has calculated that the money to be made out of his wrong-doing will probably exceed the damages at risk, it is necessary for the law to show that it cannot be broken with impunity. This category is not confined to moneymaking in the strict sense. It extends to cases in which the Defendant is seeking to gain at the expense of the [claimant] some object,—perhaps some property which he covets,—which either he could not obtain at all or not obtain except at a price greater than he wants to put down. Exemplary damages can properly be awarded whenever it is necessary to teach a wrongdoer that tort does not pay.' (at 1227)

Of this, Lord Hailsham said, in *Cassell:* 'Even a casual reading of the above passage shows that the sentence: "Where a defendant with a cynical disregard for a [claimant's] rights has calculated that the money to be made out of his wrongdoing will probably exceed the damages at risk, it is necessary for the law to show that it cannot be broken with impunity" is not intended to be exhaustive but illustrative, and is not intended to be limited to the kind of mathematical calculations to be found on a balance sheet.' (at 1078–1079).

Having specified the two categories of case for which exemplary/punitive damages may be appropriate, Lord Devlin identified three considerations that should always be borne in mind when considering an award.

First, a claimant cannot recover such damages unless he is the victim of the relevant behaviour:

> The [non-compensatory] anomaly inherent in exemplary damages would become an absurdity if a [claimant] totally unaffected by some oppressive conduct which the jury wished to punish obtained a windfall in consequence. (at 1227)

Second: while exemplary damages can be used 'in defence of liberty', they can also be used against it. Judges should be alert to ensure that they are not abused in this way.

> Some of the awards that juries have made in the past seem to me to amount to a greater punishment than would be likely to be incurred if the conduct were criminal; and moreover a

---

the police.... and almost as certainly to local and other officials exercising improperly rights of search or arrest without warrant, and it may be that in the future it will be held to include other abuses of power without warrant by persons purporting to exercise legal authority. What it will not include is the simple bully, not because the bully ought not to be punished in damages, for he manifestly ought, but because an adequate award of compensatory damages by way of solatium will necessarily have punished him. I am not prepared to say without further consideration that a private individual misusing legal powers of private prosecution or arrest..., might not at some future date be assimilated into the first category. I am not prepared to make an exhaustive list of the emanations of government which might or might not be included. But I see no reason to extend it beyond this field, to simple outrage, malice or contumelious behaviour...'

> punishment imposed without the safeguard which the criminal law gives to an offender. I should not allow the respect which is traditionally paid to an assessment of damages by a jury to prevent me from seeing that the weapon is used with restraint. It may even be that the House may find it necessary to. . . .place some arbitrary limit on awards of damages that are made by way of punishment. Exhortations to be moderate may not be enough. (at 1227–1228)

Third: the means of the parties, which are irrelevant when compensation is assessed, are material in assessing exemplary damages. 'Everything which aggravates or mitigates the Defendant's conduct is relevant.' (at 1230)

Summarising the effect of these directions, Lord Devlin said:

> In a case in which exemplary damages are appropriate, a jury should be directed that if, but only if, the sum which they have in mind to award as compensation (which may, of course, be a sum aggravated by the way in which the defendant has behaved to the plaintiff) is inadequate to punish him for his outrageous conduct, to mark their disapproval of such conduct and to deter him from repeating it, then it can award some larger sum. (at 1230)

Lord Hailsham, in *Cassell,* noted the varying terms used to denote exemplary/punitive damages. In doing so he illuminated helpfully the psychology and policy behind such awards (some of which comment apply to damages for defamation too):

> In my view it is desirable to drop the use of the phrase "vindictive" damages altogether. . . . Even when a purely punitive element is involved, vindictiveness is not a good motive for awarding punishment. In awarding "aggravated" damages the natural indignation of the court at the injury inflicted on the [claimant] is a perfectly legitimate motive in making a generous rather than a more moderate award to provide an adequate solatium. But that is because the injury to the [claimant] is actually greater and, as the result of the conduct exciting the indignation, demands a more generous solatium.
>
> Likewise the use of "retributory" is objectionable because it is ambiguous. It can be used to cover both aggravated damages to compensate the [claimant] and punitive or exemplary damages purely to punish the defendant or hold him up as an example.
>
> As between "punitive" or "exemplary," one should, I would suppose, choose one to the exclusion of the other, since it is never wise to use two quite interchangeable terms to denote the same thing. Speaking for myself, I prefer "exemplary," not because "punitive" is necessarily inaccurate, but "exemplary" better expresses the policy of the law as expressed in the cases. It is intended to teach the defendant and others that "tort does not pay" by demonstrating what consequences the law inflicts rather than simply to make the defendant suffer an extra penalty for what he has done, although that does, of course, precisely describe its effect. (at 1073)

Exemplary/punitive damages must be distinguished from aggravated damages, which are wholly compensatory in nature. Exemplary/punitive damages look to the conduct of the defendant: aggravated damages look to the effect on the claimant of the way in which the defendant conducted herself. The Law Commission (1997) characterised aggravated damages as follows: '. . .aggravated damages compensate the victim of a wrong for mental distress (or 'injury to feelings') in circumstances in which that injury has been caused or increased by the manner in which the defendant committed the wrong, or by the defendant's conduct subsequent to the wrong.'

This fairly detailed account of the principles underlying punitive and exemplary damages should not obscure the fact that such damages are unusual, anomalous, not awarded in many jurisdictions precisely because they are thought not to represent a legitimate function of the law of tort, and subject on those grounds to strenuous academic (e.g. Anderson 1992; cp Reed 1996)) and sometimes judicial criticism (Lord Denning in *Cassell v Broome* [1972] AC 1027).

The (incidentally) punitive effect of orders for costs should not be forgotten. Costs orders often dwarf awards of damages, and may often be the real punishment for a tort, and the prospect of such costs orders the real deterrent to the tort that might lead to them—assuming that the tortfeasor, as opposed to an insurance company, will pay.

The focus of this book is on the law as an agent of individual moral betterment.

Notwithstanding our concerns about the efficacy of tort in achieving appeasement, justice, and punishment, and deterrence, we acknowledge that these aims may in some cases, if realised, tend to the moral improvement of the parties. We have already observed that appeasement and punishment are inevitable desires, and may be good desires on the part of the claimant, and the facilitation of a mechanism for the realization of good desires presumably is to the moral good of the claimant. Even if a desire for appeasement/punishment is itself merely vindictive (and despite the judicial deprecation of mere vindictiveness as a basis for punitive damages), vindication may allow a claimant to move on and to abandon bad feelings—moves that are likely to improve future ethical decision-making. Appeasement and punishment may be part of a desire for justice (justice conceived widely—and more widely than the law of tort aspires to conceive it) and where that is so, it is hard to criticise those impulses as morally undesirable. But all that said, we tend to the view that appeasement and the desire for punishment are *generally* (and with many important exceptions), unlikely to help claimants become morally better. It is better to forgive or, if that is impossible or unjust, to delegate the business of retribution to the state rather than to pursue it in a private law claim—however much of a public law reality that claim may be.

That deals with appeasement, punishment and deterrence insofar as it relates to the morality of claimants. What about defendants? It seems hard to argue that the successful achievement of appeasement and/or punishment and/or deterrence will generally conduce to the moral improvement of defendants, although in individual cases they certainly might. The existence of *any* system of calling wrongfully acting or defaulting defendants to account may have moral corollaries, but generally, as we will discuss, only insofar as the act or default in question has some sort of ethical flavour. And, generally, the moral influence of a tort system on defendants will be mediated through the deterrent and compensatory elements of that system.

We have dealt in very general terms with objectives of the tort system other than compensation, but there is almost universal agreement, in which we join, that the main purpose of tort is (rightly) to compensate damage: to repair, insofar as money or any other tortious remedy can, the damage done by a tortfeasor. With the exception of punitive damages, the only other obvious exception in the civil law to the principle that compensation is the main objective is the law relating to unjust enrichment. Our main reasons for advocating compensation as the mainspring of the law of tort are our misgivings, already expressed, about the ability of tort to do anything else well, and our conviction that revenge and punishment are best seen as the business of society, rather than individuals, and hence that the criminal law is the best medium for those legitimate objectives.

To take further our examination of the shortcomings and advantages of the law of tort as a moral agent we need to look at the substantive law of that quintessential tort, negligence.

3.5 Can the Tort of Negligence be a Moral Agent?

To prove negligence the claimant must prove that the defendant owed her a duty, that the duty has been breached, and that the breach caused loss or damage of a sort recognised by the law.

The classical statement of the circumstances in which a duty is owed is the formulation of Lord Atkin in *Donoghue v Stevenson* [1932] AC 562, 580:

> The rule that you are to love your neighbour becomes in law: You must not injure your neighbour and the lawyer's question: Who is my neighbour? receives a restricted reply. You must take reasonable care to avoid acts or omissions which you can reasonably foresee would be likely to injure your neighbour. Who then in law is my neighbour? The answer seems to be persons who are so closely and directly affected by my act that I ought reasonably to have them in contemplation as being so affected when I am directing my mind to the acts or omissions which are called into question.

The very language of duties seems moral. Many jurisdictions with apparently satisfactory civil law systems have no such notion. Duties often have moral content. The impression of a *moral* formulation survives a first look at Lord Atkin's criteria. The Biblical allusion is resonant, even if Lord Atkin stresses that the obligation is not as demanding as that felt by the Good Samaritan. The reference to 'having [another] in contemplation' is similar to the lay idea of thoughtfulness. *Donoghue v Stevenson was* revolutionary. It imposed a new general duty where previously there had been clearly demarcated categories of potential liability, and in doing so it presupposed, and helped to create, connections of legal significance and potential moral significance between everyone in society—or at least between those people who had the necessary proximity with one another. It re-drew the lawyer's pictures of the person and of society and of the relationship between the two.

But, as the subsequent evolution of the law showed, Lord Atkin had expressed himself in too revolutionary a way for many—and in particular for insurers. Foreseeability of damage was the touchstone of his test, and yet many plainly foreseeable types of damage were subsequently deemed to be irrecoverable. Pure economic loss is often foreseeable, and yet (except in the special case of pure financial loss resulting from a negligent misstatement upon which the claimant has relied: see *Hedley Byrne v Heller* [1964] AC 465), is irrecoverable. Nervous shock resulting from injury to another is often foreseeable, but there are very restrictive rules governing claims for nervous shock (*Alcock* v. *Chief Constable of South Yorkshire* [1992] 1 AC 310).

Lord Atkin's simple and generous criterion of legal neighbourliness was replaced by a three-fold test: a duty will be owed if there is sufficient proximity, sufficient foreseeability, and if it is 'fair, just, and reasonable' to impose a duty.

The 'fair, just, and reasonable' test, in particular, has been an important vehicle for the importation into the law of tort of public policy. Because of our communitarian convictions, one might expect us to welcome the societal voice in private law debates that policy considerations might entail. But in fact the public policies to which the judges have generally appealed in delineating the boundaries of tortious duties have generally been policies with which we take issue. Here are four examples, with our comments on each.

First, it has often been said that the common law should not do the job of the legislature, and so judges should not craft a duty when Parliament has not done so. This is, of course, a big and complex debate, well outside the scope of this book, but we would simply say that bespoke common law solutions to legal problems tend to fit the complex contours of real people rather better than the off-the-peg, generic solutions produced in the Parliamentary draftsman's office and endorsed by busy and politically committed politicians.

Second, judges have often been reluctant to say that a tortious duty is fair, just, and reasonable where the effect of such a decision would be that the law of tort governs a relationship which could have been governed instead by contract. We suggest that this reluctance stems from a bias in the backgrounds of appellate judges, a disproportionate number of whom are commercial lawyers by intellectual upbringing and conviction, and that it presupposes an artificial view of the relationships between humans. Most of us do not seek, in a considered way, how our relations should be defined. Nor is it desirable that we should. Duties, as Lord Atkin said, should be a consequence merely of the fact of our membership of the type of society in which actual and metaphorical collisions between members of society can occur.

Third: it is commonly said, in arguing against the extension of tortious duties, that such an extension will result in a general increase of insurance premiums, to the detriment of all. In assessing the merits of this argument one has to compare three evils: the evil of a meritorious claimant going without a remedy, the evil of a blameworthy tortfeasor escaping the consequences of their action or inaction, and the evil of a small rise in general insurance premiums, which will have to be paid by the careful and prudent as well as by the negligent. Generally, we think, the combined weight of the first two related evils is likely to outweigh the third significantly.

Fourth: Judges have commonly said that if a particular type of duty is recognised, it will result in a court-clogging avalanche of claims. This seems to us to be a curious reason to debar claims that are thought to be otherwise meritorious. The courts exist for their users. Their sole raison d'etre is to ensure that justice is done, and if justice requires the recognition of a particular cause of action it is not satisfactory to say that recognition would mean that the courts were too busy. That is like saying that hospitals should be closed in pandemics because the clinical need is too great.

For a time it seemed as if the European Convention on Human Rights might take a role in shaping the English law of tort—at least where the law imposed a blanket immunity in relation to certain acts and defaults, and at least in relation to Article 6. But this promise (in *Osman v United Kingdom* (1998) 29 EHRR 245) proved to be unfounded. In *Z v United Kingdom* (2002) 34 EHRR 3 the Strasbourg court read *Osman* restrictively: *Z's* effect has been, to a large extent, to usher human rights law out of the tort courts. Thus in *Michael* v. *Chief Constable of South Wales Police* [2015] UKSC 2 the Supreme Court rejected the contention that Articles 2 and 3 of the ECHR should force an extension of the common law. Tort and human rights law had importantly different functions, the court held. Lord Toulson observed that 'whereas civil actions are designed essentially to compensate claimants for losses, Convention claims are intended to uphold minimum human rights standards and to vindicate those rights' (para 127). But this also meant, the Supreme Court subsequently held in *Commissioner of Police of the Metropolis* v. *DSD* [2018] UKSC 11, that considerations arising from the law of tort need not and should not inhibit the vindication of human rights: human rights and tort law flowed in different channels. Human rights litigation has become a substantively and procedurally different business from private law litigation.

While this may have unfettered human rights law in some respects, freeing it to do work that is almost always more ethically unambiguous than the law of tort, it also has the effect of restricting human rights law strictly to public authorities. Of course the ECHR and the Human Rights Act are expressed as relating only to public authorities, but before *Z v United Kingdom* human rights law, deployed in private law proceedings against public authorities, infused into the private law more generally, meaning that even when the defendant was not a public authority, its obligations might be read in some respects as if it were. For that reason we lament the decision in *Z v United Kingdom.*

In many circumstances where common decency and compassion would seem to require a particular course of conduct the law, desperately reluctant to compel positive action as opposed to giving a remedy for culpable inaction, does not do so. Thus there is in the English law no general duty of safe rescue or duty to warn of an obvious danger (See *Stovin v Wise* [1996] AC 923 and *Smith v Littlewoods Organisation* [1978] AC 241).

We have criticised the restricted circumstances in which the law of tort imposes duties. But when the law does impose duties, those duties often have little *moral* character. The substantive law of tort is rarely interested in states of mind (assault/battery, trespass generally, and false imprisonment are unusual examples which point up the general rule[3]). Although it may be said that some degrees or types of tortious fault are morally blameworthy, there are many examples of the law imposing liability for non-faults—such as strict vicarious liability (usually a creature of statute).

---

[3]In trespass/assault/battery the relevant state of mind is simply that the relevant act constituting interference was willed.

Even where duties are morally impeccable and, when enforced by the courts, tend to the moral betterment of society, these ethical outcomes are often frustrated by the other elements of a successful claim—the need to prove breach of duty and to prove causation of a type of loss recognised by the law.

Questionable decisions about breach of duty are less common than they were. In clinical negligence cases breach of duty is decided by reference to the test in *Bolam v Friern Management Committee* [1957] 1 WLR 582: the claimant must prove that the defendant's action or inaction would not be endorsed by a responsible body of opinion in the relevant specialty. That test was abused by defendants and misunderstood by the courts, leading to many situations where a defendant would escape if an expert could be found to say simply that, eccentric though the defendant may have been, there may be some other clinicians who would act similarly eccentrically. This was really a failure to recognise that the word 'responsible' appears in the test. The case of *Bolitho v City and Hackney Health Authority* [1997] 4 All ER 771 reminded practitioners and the courts of the presence of the word, with the result that the opinions of experts as to what constitutes responsible practice should be interrogated and can be rejected if they do not stand up to logical scrutiny. The fact that a practice is adopted by some doctors is not conclusive proof that it is responsible.

As to causation, a frequent occurrence in clinical negligence litigation is that the defendant is found to be have been in breach of duty, but the claimant fails to prove causation—resulting in a blameworthy defendant getting its costs paid by the claimant. There may be other remedies in such cases (such as a reference to a regulatory body), but unless one's idea of morality includes a rigorously scientific view of causation, such cases damage tort law's claim to be a moral agent.

A similar comment applies to the requirement to prove loss of a type recognised by the law. The classic example is nervous shock. It may have been proved that the defendant has acted negligently, and that a result of the negligence the claimant has foreseeably suffered great psychiatric distress. But in the absence of physical damage, unless the distress can be categorised as a recognised psychiatric illness, the claim will fail.

All these claim-defeating principles have, cumulatively, the effect of dulling significantly the capacity of the law of negligence to nudge individuals or groups in the direction of more ethical behaviour.

3.6 Conclusion

The last observation about the law of negligence applies almost equally to the rest of the law of tort. The only areas of *substantive* law which are partial exceptions are the law of confidentiality (which will be discussed in Chap. 6, on medical law), and the law of defamation. In the law relating to the assessment of damages, exemplary damages are a true exception.

But the general observation does not (insofar as it is true) mean that the law of tort does not promote morality. It may, taken as a whole, or constituent parts of it may, conduce to a state of society in which individual morality is more likely to thrive. One of the concerns of law generally, for instance, is certainty. It is regarded as important that people subject to the law know where they stand. So important is certainty seen to be that the law will sometimes expressly sacrifice justice, mercy, or nuance in order to ensure certainty. Certainty *may* increase societal stability. Societal stability *may* promote individual or corporate morality. Whether certainty or any of the other by-products of the law do produce stability, and whether stability does promote morality, are empirical questions beyond the scope of this book.

References

Anderson L (1992) An exemplary case for reform. Civil Just Q 11:233–260

Deakin S, Adams Z (2019) Markesinis and Deakin's Tort law, 8th edn. Oxford University Press, Oxford

Duff RA (2014) Torts, crimes and vindication: whose wrong is it? In: Dyson M (ed) Unravelling Tort and crime. Cambridge University Press, Cambridge, pp 146–173

Dyson M (2014) Tortious apples and criminal oranges. In: Dyson M (ed) Unravelling Tort and crime. Cambridge University Press, Cambridge

Law Commission (1997) Aggravated, exemplary and restitutionary damages. HMSO, London

Reed A (1996) Exemplary damages: a persuasive case for their retention as a mechanism of retributive justice. Civil Just Q 15:130–140

Unknown (1754BC, 2011) The Code of Hammurabi, Internet sacred text archive. Evinity Publishing

Chapter 4
Family Law

Abstract This chapter explores the role family law has in promoting good behaviour. It highlights three particular ways it does this. First, by providing a structure which encourages people to enter intimate relationships by ensuring that there is protection from physical and economic disadvantage. Second, by valuing and recognising the worth of caretaking. And third, by encouraging parents to promote the welfare of their children and to understand their role as involving responsibilities, rather than rights.

Keywords Family · Marriage · Cohabitation · Care · Parenthood · Financial orders · Parental responsibility

4.1 Introduction

In this chapter we explore the ways in which family law can make people good. We realise that this is a potentially dangerous claim. Family law has a sorry history of trying to do precisely this. In the past, with lingering effects, family law has privileged certain family forms, especially the heterosexual married family, and denigrated other family forms. Family law has justified horrific acts such as marital rape, domestic abuse and the physical punishment of children, as permissible exercises of the power of a husband or parent. But it need not be like that. Those harmful effects have been gradually reduced over the years, with, for example, marriage being opened up to same-sex couples, legislative reforms to tackle domestic abuse, and limitations on corporal punishment.

Our claim in this chapter is that family law is an essential framework within which people can experience the good of relationships. Indeed it would be hard to have a good relationship without the protective structures of family law. Ideally the relationship will never need the interventions of family law. Like a cam for rock climbers: you hope you don't need it but if you do you are glad you had it, and without it rock climbing is too frightening to be fun. We make three points in particular in this chapter.

© The Author(s), under exclusive license to Springer Nature Switzerland AG 2021

C. Foster, J. Herring, *The Law as a Moral Agent*, SpringerBriefs in Law,
https://doi.org/10.1007/978-3-030-71334-8_4

First: intimate relationships in our society, and perhaps any society, create inequalities. In economic terms, one party will often have benefited more than the other. If there is no remedy to rectify the unequal distribution of the gains and losses people will be pressured to ensure during their relationships that they are not being financially disadvantaged by the relationships. This is unrealistic and burdensome. Providing a mechanism at the end of the relationship to ensure a fair sharing permits someone in a relationship to make sacrifices, confident that if necessary and possible, recompense will be made if the relationship comes to an end. Everyday examples of the kind of decisions that can be made, courtesy of the remedial power of family law, without having to be extremely concerned by their long-term economic consequences, might be one spouse taking more time off work than the other to deal with childcare responsibilities, or where a family moves so that one spouse can take up a highly desirable job offer, even though the other spouse will lose their current job as a result.

Second, family law is able to value the care of children and other dependents. Caring is notoriously undervalued in legal and societal terms (Herring 2013). Family law is one of the few areas of the law where its importance is acknowledged. As caring is good, this is an example of family law encouraging people to be good.

Third, a central aspect of family law is "messaging". Through labels and accessible messaging the law is able to convey important *guidance* as to how people should behave. Many of the key principles that people seek to live their family life by are those promoted by the law: parenthood should be seen as a matter of responsibility not right; decisions about children should put the child's welfare first, and spouses and partners should be seen as equal.

4.2 Enabling and Encouraging Relationships

Family law seeks to promote various kinds of relationships. It does this by providing social recognition, through formal acknowledgement, of certain kinds of relationships, and indeed through not providing formal acknowledgement of other relationships. It also promotes the approved relationship with legal regulation and protection: this creates an attractive background against which to enter intimate relationships. In the past approved relationships were acknowledged by financial advantages, such as tax credits. Still today married couples receive tax advantages which unmarried couples do not, such as marriage allowance for income tax[1] and exemption for spousal transfers for inheritance tax.

Society's attitude towards kinds of relationships can be reflected in their legal position. Take the example of same-sex relationships. It is possible to detect a gradual progression in the law from sexual acts between couples of the same sex

[1] At the time of writing for the narrow categories of couples to whom it can apply it is worth between £351 and £907.50.

being criminal offences, to the decriminalisation of same-sex sexual activity, to limited acknowledgement that same sex couples may have particular rights in particular contexts, to a broader acceptance of the idea that discrimination law should apply to same sex couples; to same sex couples being granted a status analogous to, but distinct from marriage (civil partnerships in English law); to marriage being opened up to same sex couples. These gradual changes in legal status reflect changing social attitudes moving from abhorring, to tolerating, to embracing same-sex relationships.

Politicians from across the political spectrum are keen to be seen as "family friendly" and supportive of "hard working families". The message seems clear: well done for being in a family—especially a marriage.

But here's the rub. Promoting families may imply a denigration of those groupings which are not familial. This is a common complaint about marriage, and the family law which promotes and protects it. Family law has traditionally privileged, and to a much lesser extent still does privilege, marriages over other forms of relationship. Tax advantages, various bureaucratic benefits, legal advantages, and social recognition all preference married couples over others. This might be seen as a blatant attempt to encourage people to do the 'right thing' in their private relationships and be married, or at least be part of a family.

That leaves the question of why it is thought to be good to be married or in a family. Traditionally family law has focussed on sexual relationships, in particular those within marriage, as being the cardinal indicator of family life. Lynn Wardle (2011) expresses the traditional view:

> Marriage is the primary expression of and preferred locus for the most meaningful and socially beneficial forms of intimate belonging.

While the law has expanded the definition of which couples can get married, it still tends to see permanent, stable relationships as more or less satisfactory depending on how closely they parallel traditional heterosexual marriage. Hence there are complaints that same-sex couples must fit into the "heterosexual conception" of marriage and only unmarried couples who are "living together as if they were married" can claim certain rights. In other words traditional marriage is treated as the ideal to which other relationships must aspire. Those whose intimate relations do not fit within the traditional couple model struggle to find recognition in the law—be that a long term carer of a person with disabilities, or a polyamorous group. Susan Boyd (2013) states that marriage 'can be viewed as an ideological 'enclosure,' which prioritizes coupledom and heterosexuality, making these the norms against which all other relationships are measured.' Similarly, Elizabeth Brake (2012, p. 121) claims that marriage

> recognizes a single central exclusive relationship of a certain priority and duration [but] ignores alternative ideals of relationship: close dyadic friendships, small group family units, or networks of multiple, significant nonexclusive relationships that provide emotional support, caretaking, and intimacy.

It may be that Brake is not giving sufficient weight to the potential flexibility around the concept of marriage. As Martha Fineman (2004, p. 99) argues:

> Marriage, to those involved in one, can mean a legal tie, a symbol of commitment, a privileged sexual affiliation, a relationship of hierarchy and subordination, a means of self-fulfillment, a social construct, a cultural phenomenon, a religious mandate, an economic relationship, the preferred unit for reproduction, a way to ensure against poverty and dependence on the state, a way out of the birth family, the realization of a romantic ideal, a natural or divine connection, a commitment to traditional notions of morality, a desired status that communicates one's sexual desirability to the world, or a purely contractual relationship in which each term is based on bargaining.

Nevertheless, we getting to the nub of the issue. Are there relationships of the kind which need the promotion of the law, which are good and deserve particular protection? We believe that there are, but they are not the ones the current law focusses on. Traditionally, and still to some extent now, family law seems focused on the regulation of sexual relationships. It is too big a theme for this book to explore precisely which relationships should be promoted by the law, but as we have argued elsewhere the focus of the law should be on good caring relationships. We will not seek to justify that claim here: perhaps it is self-evident. The key point we are making in this chapter is that a legal framework is essential for enabling good caring relationships to be undertaken in a safe way, enabling their goods to be realised, and that without this legal framework such relationships would be highly risky and carry injustice. We suggest there are two aspects of family law in particular which enable caring relationships.

4.2.1 Protection from Physical Abuse

As is well known, domestic abuse is a pervasive feature of intimate relationships. The statistics are horrific. The World Health Organization (2017) reports that:

- about 1 in 3 (35%) women worldwide have experienced either physical and/or sexual intimate partner violence or non-partner sexual violence in their lifetime.
- most of this violence is intimate partner violence. Worldwide, almost one third (30%) of women who have been in a relationship report that they have experienced some form of physical and/or sexual violence by their intimate partner in their lifetime.
- globally, as many as 38% of murders of women are committed by a male intimate partner.

It has been estimated that worldwide half of all women who were killed, were killed by intimate partners or family relatives.

The risk of domestic abuse is, therefore, inherent within intimate relationships, at least within our society. Intimate relationships involve becoming physically and emotionally vulnerable. It is through our intimate relationships that we form our identity and sense of self, and so intimate abuse strikes at the victim's very conception of her self. Intimate relationship abuse, therefore, turns a relationship which should be a vehicle of for self-affirmation and self-identification into a vehicle of alienation and self-betrayal. The victim almost becomes used as a weapon against herself. When, therefore, a person enters what they believe to be an intimate relationship they are opening themselves up to the risk of intimate abuse. Family law, if it is to promote caring relationships and protect people from the wrongs of intimate abuse, must focus on caring relationships as being the ones where the protection is most required. As the Istanbul Convention indicates, to provide an effective response to domestic abuse requires an extensive range of legal and social mechanisms.

4.2.2 Protection from Economic Unfairness

It is nearly inevitable that during an intimate relationships one party will make economic gains and the other economic losses. While there has been a shift in the attitudes expressed by opposite sex couples about how they ought to share housework and childcare (Treas and Tai 2016) the reality is that men still specialize in market work while the woman focuses on non-market work such as housework or childcare. While female involvement in employment is at far higher rates than previously, that employment is often part time, and the division of housework is still unequally divided (Treas and Lui 2018). The slight reduction in the gap between men and women is caused by women doing less work, rather than men doing more (Hook 2010). Fetterolf and Rudman (2014) have estimated, looking at women in employment, that they spend an average of 24.5 h per week on housework and childcare, where for men the figure was 16.6 h. A Pew Centre study asking parents if they struggled to balance work and parenthood, found that 58% of millennial mothers said that parenthood had had a significantly negative impact on their career, while only 19% of fathers reported any impact (Treas and Lui 2018). While the couple are together and are pooling their resources this is not particularly problematic, but if the couple breaks up, without some compensation women in particular are likely to lose out.

An ideal may be a society in which these tasks are shared equally, but that is difficult in our society. Indeed, it may be, as Shari Motro (2008) argues, that:

> Marriage is not fundamentally about equal contribution of labour. It is about two people joining the risks and rewards of their lives: merging their fates, committing to be 'in the same boat,' to sink or swim together, to contribute unequally at times if that's what it takes to keep the union afloat.

This way of putting the argument is interesting. It is not precisely an agreement for recognising as equal the contributions to the relationship, but rather an agreement for sharing the joys, slings and arrows of the shared life. If that is the starting point, then when the relationship comes to an end there may be some cases where no order is needed because the disadvantages and benefits have evened out. But, particularly where caring responsibilities have resulted from the relationship, these are likely to continue well beyond its end. Then a court order equalising the consequences of the relationship would reflect the basis of the relationship and ensure that caring relationships are not a vehicle for exploitation. As Lady Hale (2011, p. 23) has asked:

> Do we want to encourage responsible families, in which people are able to compromise their place in the world outside the home for the sake of their partners, their children and their elderly or disabled relatives, and can be properly compensated for this if things go wrong? I continue to hope that we do.

One obvious response to this may be that a couple does not need family law to provide this kind of regime, but rather than rely on contracts, such as pre-nuptial agreements. The emphasis on agreement or contract is based on the assumption that we want to regulate care prospectively and persuade the parties to settle in advance their arrangements over care. However, serious relationships are journeys, with unexpected detours, missteps and joyful surprises. No one at the start can set out what will be a fair division of the assets because no one knows where the relationship will take them. And that is why it should matter little, if at all, whether the couple are married or not. It is true that normally in the law we do look for a formal promise or demonstration of commitment but this is not needed in a respectively-operating family law system where we have a far richer source of obligation—namely what has actually happened during the relationship.

These key roles for family law provide a framework within which a degree of safety and economic security can be provided for those in caring relationships—certainly to a greater extent than would be provided in a legal system without such provision. Of course, such a framework is no guarantee that abuse will not occur or economic unfairness cannot be remedied, but the law here does what it can to promote good caring relationships.

4.2.3 *Divorce*

Until very recently (the position was changed by the Divorce, Dissolution and Separation Act 2020) if a spouse were to consult a lawyer wanting a divorce, the first thing the lawyer would do (after, of course, explaining about their fees), would be to ask the client to list all the worst things that the other spouse had done to them. These would then be typed up into a draft divorce petition and sent to the other spouse. It is hard to think of a system more likely to encourage bitterness and exacerbate conflict rather than encouraging co-operation and empathy. There has been widespread criticism of this fault-based divorce, and its replacement encourages the parties not to look back and dredge up the negatives of the past, but to focus on the welfare of the children and finding a way to move on. This must be sensible. While it would be naive in the extreme to believe that this reform will dramatically reduce bitterness on divorce, at least it will not exacerbate it, and will enable the couple to try and find a positive way forward.

4.3 Valuing Care

Care is of central value and importance to our lives. It should be a central concept in the law too—recognised, valued, and protected by the law. Maxine Eichner (2010, p. 14) writes:

> Because of its interest in the health, well-being, and dignity of its citizens, the liberal state has a vital interest in the success of relationships that foster caretaking, and should provide these relationships with the institutional support that will help them flourish.

It is part of our human nature that we inevitably depend on one another. Martha Fineman (2004) argues that those who undertake the care of a dependent assume a condition of "derivative dependency": by fulfilling their caring obligations to the dependant they themselves become dependent on others. This dependency, which limits a person's autonomy and independence, must, she argues, be compensated. In many areas of law caring work goes unvalued and unacknowledged. However, family law is one of the few areas which emphasise and acknowledge the importance of care. We will emphasise three.

4.3.1 Defining Parenthood

It used to be fairly straight forward to define a parent in legal terms. The father was the person whose sperm was used to create the child and the mother was the person who provided the egg. The only difficulty was in proving those facts. For those purposes the law developed a series of presumptions, such as that the woman who gives birth to a child is the mother, and her husband the father. However, this straightforward definition has come under challenge in the last 60 years, from two main sources. First: increasingly children are raised in families involving a range of different parent figures. Step-parents, grandparents, child minders, and family friends may all play a major role in raising a child. It is increasingly rare for a child to be born to a couple who remain as the primary carers of that child throughout the child's life. This has challenged the traditional model of parenting. Second, modern technologies mean that children can be born to a couple using donated gametes, with no expectation that the providers of those gametes will play a role in the child's life. This has led to decreasing weight being attached to merely *genetic* relationships. Two alternative basis for allocating parenthood will be outlined.

Under the labour-based account, parenthood is allocated based on parental labour. It is a form of reward or compensation for the care put in. One interesting consequence of this approach is that certainly at birth the mother will be recognised as having made a greater contribution than a father, and so have a stronger parental claim. The labour-based approach does acknowledge that as the child grows other adults may engage in significant levels of care of the child and come to deserve the status of parent.

Under the welfare-based approach, parenthood should be allocated based on who will be the best parent for the child. This is normally based on who has the closest relationship with the child and who is therefore likely to make the best decision for the child. We might assume that a person who has spent most time caring for the child will have got to know them best. The strongest argument in favour of this approach is that it is closely tied to the primary legal consequence of parenthood: that a parent has the right to make decisions about a child's upbringing.

Parental status should be earned by care and dedication to the child: this is not shown simply by a biological link. It is the changing of the nappy, the wiping of the tear and the working out of maths together that make a parent, not the provision of an egg or sperm. We should give parental status and rights to those who are likely to make the best decisions for the child in question. That will be the person who knows the child best: the person who is caring for the child day to day. In this way the law can acknowledge, value and encourage the care of children.

4.3.2 Financial Orders

As already acknowledged, there is a need to ensure fair sharing of the economic advantages and disadvantages that flow from a relationship. Care work is indeed recognised and valued as something important not only to the recipient of the care, but also to the care-recipient's family community and wider society. To leave a person who has undertaken care during a relationship with no financial recognition at the end is to devalue it. By contrast the House of Lords in *White v White* [2000] UKHL 54 justified the starting point of an equal division of marital assets on the basis that the contribution through childcare and home making was as valuable as a financial contribution.

Through financial orders on divorce, determined by the values of the law, our community is able to recognize the value and importance of care work. There is much more that our society needs to do to properly value that work, but this is a start.

4.3.3 The Welfare of Children

Where there is a dispute concerning a child which a court must resolve, most jurisdictions require the court to focus on the welfare or best interests of the child. There is much that is beneficial about the welfare principle: it ensures that the focus is on the child and enables an individual assessment of the needs of the child (Herring 2005). However, children live, as we all do, in the context of relationships of care. We cannot separate either the welfare or the rights of children from those of their parents. Their interests and rights are so intertwined and the parties so interdependent that to consider what order will promote the welfare of the child, as an isolated individual, and without consideration of the interests of the parents, as the courts suggest that they do, is simply impossible.

Brighouse and Swift (2014) argue that in good parent-child relationships children become part of the life of parents and receive the care, trust, affection and intimacy of being parented in a spontaneous way. That, however, is only possible if, to some extent, the child is involved in the life of the parents. The father who enjoys watching football every Saturday is doing nothing wrong in involving his children in football-watching. Indeed, that may be part of the good of parenting is that children get caught up in the pleasures of their parents, even if in later life they eschew them. Children living with parents who laboriously seek out the best activities for children, with no thought of themselves, miss the natural spontaneity of family life. A parent seeking to engage a child in interests and hobbies which are good for the child but boring to an adult may not be conducive of a good parent-child relationship (Altman 2018).

This may explain why, in fact, the courts are far more willing to intervene in a decision about children which does not related directly to the life of the parent, such as what medical treatment a child should receive, but are reluctant to intervene in decisions which directly affect the lifestyle of parents, such as whether the family practises naturism (*Re W (Residence Order)* ([1999] 1 FLR 869).

A law centred on the importance of care would require us to consider the child in the network of relationships within which they live. Relationship-based welfare argues that children should be brought up in relationships which overall promote their welfare. It is beneficial for a child to be brought up in a family that is based on relationships which are fair and just. A relationship based on unacceptable demands on a parent is not furthering a child's welfare. Indeed, it is impossible to construct an approach to looking at a child's welfare which ignores the web of relationships within which the child is brought up. Supporting the child means supporting the caregiver and supporting the caregiver means supporting the child. So a court can legitimately make an order whose obvious and immediate benefit is to the parent, rather than the not a child. The order would have to be justified in terms of the best interests of the child, but in fact, as the courts sometimes (and increasingly) recognise, the interests of parents and children cannot be neatly distinguished.

4.4 Messaging

Family law plays a powerful role in sending messages to society which have significance beyond the formal legal significance, and can be seen to influence good behaviour and attitudes. A good example is the advent of equal marriage. In legal terms there was relatively little significance in the fact that a same-sex couple could marry as well as entering a civil partnership, as civil partnership carried, in effect, the same set of rights as marriage. But it was a powerful statement by the law that same sex couples could be regard, in terms of public understanding, as equal to opposite sex couples. Since the advent of equal marriage surveys of public opinion has shown a marked increase in support of same-sex relationships. While correlation does not prove causation, the law plays a role in shaping the public discourse.

A similar issue can be found in the debates generated by the decision in *R (McConnell) v Registrar General* [2019] EWCA Civ 599 where the question was whether a trans-man who had given birth to a child should be registered as male or female. In legal terms it mattered little: he would in any event be the parent and have parental responsibility. But the social significance and what was being said about what it was to be a mother or a father was key. The finding—that he was the mother because he had gestated the child, despite being a man for legal purposes—tied the concept of motherhood to gestation rather than gender. Whether one agrees with that finding or not, it illustrates how the law can be seen as reinforcing or shaping certain cultural norms and understandings.

A further example can be found in the concept of parental responsibility. Section 3 of the Children Act 1989 states:

> In this Act 'parental responsibility' means all the rights, duties, powers, responsibilities and authority which by law a parent of a child has in relation to the child and his property.

It is notable that English law uses the term responsibility rather than rights to describe the legal significance of the parental status. It was deliberately chosen to send the message that parents should see their role as not about exercising power over children, but rather seeking to promote their welfare. Lord Scarman in *Gillick* v *West Norfolk and Wisbech AHA* [1986] AC 112, at 184 argued that parents' rights exist only for the purpose of discharging their duties to children: 'Parental rights are derived from parental duty and exist only so long as they are needed for the protection of the person and property of the child.'

4.5 Conclusion

In this chapter we have explored three ways that family law can promote good behaviour, and in particular caring relationships. First, we argue that family law provides a necessary scaffold to protect those in intimate caring relationships. Second, family law recognises and values the importance of caring. Third, family law sends positive messages about the importance and value of care.

References

Altman S (2018) Parental control rights. In: Brake E, Ferguson L (eds) Philosophical foundations of family law. Oxford University Press, Oxford

Boyd S (2013) 'Marriage is more than just a piece of paper': feminist critiques of same sex marriage. North Taiwan Univ Law Rev 8:263–298

Brake E (2012) Minimizing marriage: marriage, morality, and the law. Oxford University Press, New York

Brighouse H, Swift A (2014) Family values: the ethics of parent-child relationships. Princeton University Press, Princeton
Eichner M (2010) The supportive state. Oxford University Press, Oxford
Fetterolf J, Rudman L (2014) Gender inequality in the home: the role of relative income, support for traditional gender roles, and perceived entitlement. Gender Issues 31:219–229
Fineman M (2004) The autonomy myth. New Press, New York
Hale B (2011) Equality and autonomy in family law. J Soc Welfare Family Law 33:3–23
Herring J (2005) Farewell welfare. J Soc Welfare Family Law 27:159–171
Herring J (2013) Caring and the law. Hart, Oxford
Hook J (2010) Gender inequality in the welfare state: sex segregation in housework, 1965–2003. Am Sociol Rev 115:480–492
Motro S (2008) Labor, luck, and love: reconsidering the sanctity of separate property. Northwest Univ Law Rev 102:1623–1678
Treas J, Lui J (2018) Studying housework across nations. J Family Theory Rev 5:135–151
Treas J, Tai T (2016) Gender inequality in housework across 20 European nations: lessons from gender stratification theories. Sex Roles 75:495–512
Wardle L (2011) The boundaries of belonging: allegiance, purpose and the definition of marriage. Brigham Young Univ Public Law 25:287–315
World Health Organization (2017) Violence against women. WHO, Geneva

Chapter 5
Criminal Law

Abstract This chapter explores the role of criminal law in making people good. It highlights three particular aspects. First, the criminal justice system can be seen as engaging the defendant in a moral conversation to determine whether or not they are responsible for their actions, and if they are, the appropriate response to any wrongdoing. Conviction and punishment are designed to restore the defendant to membership of the moral community. Second, the criminal law is limited in its reach. This is a deliberate limitation, designed to enable people to act virtuously and do good. Third, through the criminal law, the state constitutes itself as a protector of citizen's rights and frees people to engage in good behaviour.

Keywords Censure · Crime · Punishment · Repentance · Domestic abuse

5.1 Introduction

To many criminal lawyers the suggestion that the criminal law can or should be used to make people good will be met with a sigh. We have been there, done that, and moved on. Yes, in more primitive times, or in oppressive regimes, it is seen as appropriate to use the criminal law to enforce a moral code, but in a modern secular multi-cultural society we don't do that. Indeed, where moralism is used in the literature it is often used as a form of criticism of a particular viewpoint. Hyman Gross (2012, p. viii), for example, has dedicated a book to support the claim that "while crimes may indeed be morally wrong, it is a source of mischief for theory and practice to deal with them as such under the law".

It will be argued in this chapter that, in fact, making people good is a key feature of criminal law. Clearly, it is right to reject the idea that we can compel people to be good through threats of punishment. The most that might be said is that such a law will stop people being really bad. That is not something to be sneezed at. There is certainly some credit in being able to say one lived a life without doing anything bad. But there is much more to the criminal law's efforts to make people good. Three of its strategies will be outlined in this chapter. First, criminal justice process uses censure, dialogue and rehabilitation as a process to make people good. Second, the refusal to

© The Author(s), under exclusive license to Springer Nature Switzerland AG 2021

C. Foster, J. Herring, *The Law as a Moral Agent*, SpringerBriefs in Law,
https://doi.org/10.1007/978-3-030-71334-8_5

criminalise some behaviour, such as failing to rescue someone in peril, enables moral behaviour. Third, criminal law prohibitions are essential for creating an environment in which good lives are lived.

5.2 Criminal Trials, Convictions and Punishment as a Moral Conversation

Anthony Duff (2001, p. 115) has set out the moral role for the criminal law:

> Criminal punishment . . . should communicate to offenders the censure they deserve for their crimes, and should aim through that communicative process to persuade them to repent their crimes, to try to reform themselves, and thus to reconcile themselves with those whom they wronged.

In broad terms that is an approach we adopt. Of course, in plenty of cases such attempts do not work and there is no "repentance" or "reconciliation", but it is a goal a state should achieve and is a powerful route to making people better. It is worth breaking down the different aspects of this process.

5.2.1 Censure

Censure attaches to a criminal conviction. When a person is convicted of a criminal offence, there is a particular kind of censure taking place: a moral judgement, expressed by society (Von Hirsch 1996). This can be seen in the different reactions to learning that a friend had been required to pay £1000 in a dispute over a contract, and discovering they had been ordered to pay a fine of £1000 in a criminal case. At one level the impact of the court order is the same: the friend is liable to pay the £1000, but the message sent by the order is very different. From the former there would no reason to assume that your friend had done anything that might be questionable in terms of moral principle. There may have been a legitimate dispute over the correct interpretation of a contract, or they may have been unable, through no fault of their own, to fulfil a contractual obligation. A fine, by contrast, would involve a clear implication that your friend had done something morally wrong. It is through the criminal trial that an assessment is made as to whether this censure is appropriate and in the punishment that the response to the censure is affected.

Not everyone agrees with this. Hyman Gross (2012, p. xiii) complains that the link between a conviction and censure has "the unfortunate effect of giving support to regressive tendencies in the public domain by encouraging the belief that criminal justice is some sort of exercise in righteousness". Such a view is problematic because it is hard to imagine a criminal law that is free of morality. As Yongjae Lee (2015), in a review of Gross's book notes:

> Gross believes that we should avoid punishing the innocent, refrain from punishing disproportionately, respect the principle that crimes of different seriousness should be punished at different levels, and avoid differential treatments of crimes of same seriousness. It is unclear, however, how he proposes that we respect all these principles without engaging in the kind of moral reasoning that he condemns throughout the book.

Indeed, it is hard to imagine how one could fashion, say, a law on rape, that contained no assessment of moral wrongdoing. Notably Gross (2012, p. 66) himself slips into moralistic language in his discussion of rape, criticising one view as "morally impoverished". It seems almost unavoidable that a message of moral blame attaches to a criminal conviction.

5.2.2 *What Is Censured?*

It is important to be clear about what the censure theory is saying. First, it is clear that the criminal law is not seeking to punish all wrongful conduct. Duff (2018) has supported what he called "negative legal moralism": we should not punish conduct unless it is wrongful. That is different, of course, from saying that all behaviour which is wrongful is criminalised. There are plenty of examples to show that it would be absurd to seek to do that: criminalising unpunctuality would be one. The criminalisation contains a message that the behaviour is wrongful; not that all behaviour which is not criminal is morally permitted! Everyone knows that, or they should.

Second, the criminal law is not saying that something is criminal *only* because it is wrongful. It is obvious that there are considerations impacting criminalisation other than wrongfulness: the economic impact on society without a criminal offence, whether the offence can be proved in court, and whether the wrong is too trivial are all factors to take into account. Indeed this is made clear in the Code for Crown Prosecutors (CPS 2018) which requires prosecutors to decide before bringing a case whether or not it is in the public interest to do so.

From these points it becomes clear that the censure attaching to a criminal conviction is identifying not just a wrong per se, but a particular kind of wrong. In the literature the language of "public wrong" is commonly used to identify the kinds of moral wrongdoing that require the censure of the criminal law, with private wrongs being better dealt informally between individuals or within community settings. Hence, Duff (2018, p. 233) argues:

> 1. We have reason to criminalize a type of conduct if, and only if, it constitutes a public wrong.
> 2. A type of conduct constitutes a public wrong if, and only if, it violates the polity's civil order.

So, to give a straightforward example, if your friend forgets an arrangement to meet for coffee, that is clearly a private matter between the two of you which can, hopefully, be quickly resolved by an apology. There is no need for state involvement in the matter: indeed this is nowhere near being the kind of wrong for which criminal law censure is appropriate. We reserve criminal proceedings for public wrongs.

However, there are dangers with the language of "public wrong". As Anthony Duff and Susan Marshall (1998, p. 21) write:

> If we ask why such wrongs as murder, rape, and theft should be crimes, the natural answer is not that such actions threaten "the social order" or "the public interest": for such answers seem to ignore, and thus to denigrate, what the individual victim has suffered, and to (mis)portray crimes simply as acts of bad citizenship. The answer is, rather, that such wrongs injure important *Rechtsgüter*: the state has a duty to use the criminal law to promote respect for such significant individual rights. Such a perspective can also ground the demands, which have become more strident in recent years, that victims of crime should be allowed a more prominent, personal role in the criminal process, particularly in sentencing: since the offender's punishment is owed primarily, if not only, to those he has wronged, they should surely have a voice in determining that punishment.

From such a perspective the criminal law is both responding to the harm to society and acting on behalf of the victim. Not all commentators agree with that approach. Grant Lamond (2007), by contrast, sees the criminal law as dealing with wrongs which the community is responsible for punishing. For him it is not a question of whether the wrong is public or private, but rather whether the punishment of the wrong should be seen as the job of the community. This seems a preferable approach for two reasons. First, the victim may not wish to "share" their wrong with the state. A good example might be a victim of domestic abuse who does not wish to share the proceedings to be brought. There might be good reasons to proceed with the prosecution nonetheless. The example of domestic abuse also highlights the difficulty of separating private and public harms, as in those cases the cases involve complex mixtures of both.

So, we can be clear that appropriate criminal censure attaches to morally wrong acts, of the kind which need the criminal intervention of the state.

5.2.3 Treating the Defendant as a Moral Agent

The fact of state censure is an acknowledgment that the defendant is a moral agent. One of the reasons we try humans but not non-human animals is that (maybe mistakenly) we assume that humans, but not non-humans, are capable of moral reasoning, and hence accountable for their actions. Further, that is why, at least, for all serious crimes a mental element is required. Hence in R v *G and R* [2003] UKHL 50, para 32 the House of Lords explained:

> it is a salutary principle that conviction of serious crime should depend on proof not simply that the defendant caused (by act or omission) an injurious result to another but that his state of mind when so acting was culpable. This, after all, is the meaning of the familiar rule *actus non facit reum nisi mens sit rea*. The most obviously culpable state of mind is no doubt an intention to cause the injurious result, but knowing disregard of an appreciated and unacceptable risk of causing an injurious result or a deliberate closing of the mind to such risk would be readily accepted as culpable also.

In that case the conviction of two boys 11 and 12 on the basis that an reasonable adult would have foreseen the risk, even though it was not shown they did, was overturned on the basis it was not shown they were aware of the risk. Similarly the criminal law has a range of defences which are primarily designed to ensure that the defendant was responsible for their actions and not, for example, acting under duress or as a result of a mental disorder.

Anthony Duff (2007) in his book *Answering for Crime* explains that we should understand criminal responsibility "as a matter of being responsible (ie answerable) *for* something, *to* some person or body, within a responsibility-ascribing practice." This means that the criminal trial is a profoundly moral exercise. The defendant in the criminal law system is entitled to give an account which explains why what they did was not wrong or not an act for which they can be held responsible. It recognises that (generally) human are people who act for reasons and can be required to give an account of those reasons. Not to be so accountable, to be driven by forces outside your control, is not a desirable state. If we do not hold to account, we treat the person as someone who has no control over their destiny or is unable to respond to moral reasons. That would be a form of disrespect. As Christopher Bennett (2019) argues

> there are some contexts in which we owe it to a person to respond to him in ways that hold him to account for what he has done. If, in these contexts, one simply treated the offender as a danger to be neutralised one would then be failing to treat him as one should – one would be failing to see him and deal with him in the way that should have been most salient in that context, i.e. as an accountable agent.

He goes on to explain:

> In order to do that we would need a sympathetic articulation of the meaning and value of our practices of accountability: for example, of what underpins our sense that people ought to apologise for their wrongful actions; that they can stand in need of forgiveness before everyday business with them can be resumed; that reactions like distancing or, by contrast, angry confrontation, can be necessary when the wrongdoer is not prepared to apologise and try to put things right.

In a sense the criminal trial can be seen as a moral conversation. It encourages the defendant to think about what they did and whether there is any justification or excuse for what they did (Levanon 2019). It asks them to accept moral accountability for what they have done. This dialogue means that, as Duff puts it, the criminal law " addresses potential offenders not as outsiders, whose membership of the normative community is thus cast in doubt, but as fellow members of that community." But it also means, as Hannah Maslen (2017) has emphasised, that it is important that the state responds to the communication of the defendant. This might entail reducing a sentence because of remorse expressed, or assessing the strength of a defence raised. She explains:

> [T]he term 'dialogue' … is *responsive* – what is communicated by participant A is influenced by the prior communication of participant B, with a view to his subsequent response … it necessarily involves *attention to one's interlocutor* – one is not involved in dialogue if one ignores the other participant's input.

In this way the state is encouraging citizens to think morally about their behaviour. It also indicates in the criminal law the kinds of factors which might or might not be seen as acceptable as an excuse or justification for behaviour.

The conversation does not end with the trial. It continue during the punishment. As Andrew Von Hirsch (1996) explains

> The disapproval conveyed by the sanction gives the actor the opportunity to reconsider his actions and to feel shame or regret. However, it is left to him to respond. Censure . . . need not specifically be fashioned to elicit certain sentiments in him – whether those be shame, repentance or whatever.

This is the morally appropriate response. Forcing a display of regret is not achieving anything morally effective for the defendant him or herself. So it is right that the court process and punishment gives the opportunity for the defendant to reflect on and regret what has happened, but also right that the defendant's response is not compelled. As John Tasioulas (2006) writes:

> The offender is intended to understand the censure conveyed by the criminal sanction, and hopefully to endorse the condemnation it expresses, to experience remorse and eventually come to repent of his wrong-doing by willingly undergoing the punishment meted out to him as a justified penance. As the ideal upshot of this process, the offender will go on to reform his future behaviour and attitudes so that he can achieve some kind of reconciliation with both his victim and the wider community whose norms he has violated.

There are rich themes here but they all demonstrate that in the criminal law accountability can be conceived as to do with a moral conversation—one in which the state, citizens and community hold each other to account and seek to promote goodness.

5.2.4 The Constitutive Role of the Criminal Justice System

The prosecution of moral wrongs is a characteristic of a good society. A good society, like a good person, needs in appropriate circumstances to "call out" the wrongdoing of those and to acknowledge the harm done to others. Sometimes silence in the face of a wrongdoing is to acquiesce or even condone. Condemnation of wrongdoing is justifiable when the person condemning has the authority and resources to correctly condemn the behaviour—which the state generally does have through the criminal justice system. Of course condemnation must be treated with care. But the state with a formal legal system is particularly well placed with to put in place checks to ensure that its censure is appropriate and evidence-based. Not all censures by individuals are: they may be (for instance) manifestations of individual guilt, or letting off steam, or attempts to assert moral superiority. Through prosecution and criminal trials the state seeks to foster a better society and protect other potential victims. In public condemnation the state is acknowledging the wrong done to the victim; making it clear to all that the wrong will not be accepted by society; that the behaviour is not something that "just happens". It is an acknowledgement that the wellbeing of individuals matters to society as a whole, and is not just a matter for the victim to deal with on their own. As Duff and Marshall (1998, p. 20) write:

> A group can ... 'share' the wrongs done to its individual members, insofar as it defines and identifies itself as a community united by mutual concern, by genuinely shared ... values and interests, and by the shared recognition that its members' goods (and their identity) are bound up with their membership of the community. Wrongs done to individual members of the community are then wrongs against the whole community ... insofar as the individual goods which are attacked are goods in terms of which the community identifies and understands itself.

A failure to respond to the wrong would be letting the victim down. We might have wished we could have stopped the victim being harmed, but if we cannot do that we should condemn what was done to them. In responding to violence with moral condemnation the state is expressing itself as a moral entity. As Michelle Madden Dempsey (2011) writes concerning domestic violence:

> when a patriarchal polity condemns patriarchal violence it reconstitutes itself as less patriarchal. In order to realize this (re)constitutive value, the polity must act on its own behalf, for its own reasons, and not merely on behalf of the victim It is (in part) because the criminal justice officials act as representatives of their communities—rather than merely as representatives of the individual victims—that they are particularly well-positioned to realize the value of reconstituting the character of their communities in these valuable ways.

5.2.5 How the Criminal Justice System Could Work Better

There are certainly some challenges to the criminal law if it seeks to take on that role. The first is the binary crudity of the outcome of the criminal process: guilty or not guilty. Proper moral accountability may require a more nuanced response to this. John Gardner (2007, p. 133) has argued that not to hold people responsible for their actions is to deny self-respect:

> Self-respect is an attitude which everyone ought to have if they deserve it, and which, moreover, everyone ought to deserve. The self-respecting person aspires to live up to the proper standards for success in and fitness for the life she leads, and holds herself out to be judged by those standards. It follows that it is part of the nature of self-respect that a self-respecting person wants to be able to give an intelligible rational account of herself, to be able to show that her actions were the actions of someone who aspired to live up to the proper standards for success in her life and fitness to lead it. She wants it to be the case that her actions were not truly wrongful, of if they were wrongful, that they were at any rate justified, or if they were not justified, that they were at any rate excused. A denial of responsibility rules all of this out, and there is, accordingly, the line of defence which counts as an admission of defeat for any self-respecting person.

We fear that Gardner overstates his point here. A person lacking mental capacity, and so not fully responsible for their action, does not as a result lose the right to self-respect. His comments also suggests a somewhat inflated vision of our capacities: we are not all heroic souls who occupy a philosophical Olympus. It also seems there should be room to claim a *partial* responsibility for one's behaviour—to acknowledge that it would have been significantly harder for X than other people to meet the standard demanded by society. Yet the criminal law is rather blunted in its acknowledgment of the legitimacy of a claim of partial responsibility.

In an article one of us (JH) co-wrote with the great Alan Bogg (Bogg and Herring 2010), we considered the issue of responsibility for crimes committed by addicts. In that article we considered the 12 steps promoted by Alcoholics Anonymous to explore conceptions of responsibility for addiction. We observed that the legal and ethical debates around addiction tend to oscillate between those who see addiction is an illness, which deserves no blame, and those who see it as a moral failing, for which the defendant is responsibility. We noted that:

> On a superficial reading of the 12 steps, it might be thought that the model draws a neat connection between 'disease' and denial of responsibility. For example, step 1 refers to the addict being 'powerless' over alcohol or addiction and step 2 the need for a restoration of the addict's 'sanity'. However, the overall tenor of the 12 steps is rooted in a call to moral responsibility for the addict. Step 5 envisages a moral inventory of 'wrongs' perpetrated by the addict whilst engaged in active addiction. This seems to be based upon an understanding of the addict as *responsible* in some way for those wrongs. This is reinforced by the structure of steps 8 and 9 where the addict must make restorative amends for 'harm' done whilst addicted.... The alcoholic's recovery lies in the shedding of these vices and character defects, and the corresponding cultivation of virtuous dispositions. Only then will the character-based causes of the *disease* of alcoholism be addressed and the compulsion to drink lifted.

The journey of the 12 steps seeks to combine an acknowledgement of powerlessness and a duty to accept responsibility. As we note in the article, this is a more sophisticated middle route than the crude responsible/non-responsible dichotomy of the criminal law. It acknowledges the addict's need for love, support and fellowship; while also noting that holding the addict to account is an important part of the route to recovery. It is not, however, beyond the wit of criminal law to develop a more nuanced approach. The diminished responsibility defence acknowledges partial responsibility, but is limited to charges of murder. If the criminal law is to rely on the kind of moral conversation advocated above, it needs to develop some more sophisticated responses to cases of partial responsibility.

The state also needs to try to ensure that, at the end of the punishment, the offender is given appropriate opportunities to resume his/her life as a citizen of the society in question (Canton 2019).

Then, as Antje Du Bois-Pedain (2017) writes:

> ... To punish means to engage with the offender, and that means that *it can and must always be asked what treating the offender in this or that way says about yourself.*

The criminal justice system does little to encourage the state to examine itself and understand what responsibility, if any, *it* bears. Interestingly coroners' inquests, using narrative verdicts and with a focus on broader lessons to be learned, can be much more effective in this regard (Bottoms 2019).

5.2.6 *Conclusion on the Communicative Nature of Criminal Justice*

We accept that what has just been said can sound hopelessly idealistic. The idea that in a busy magistrates court concerned mainly with handing out fines for shoplifting and driving offences there is much by way of a "moral conversation" is the worst kind of ivory tower-ism. It is true, too, that there are plenty of sneering defendants who would find such an idea amusing. That this is true is not concerning. The criminal process can, and should, attempt some kind of conversation. It should aspire to the kind imagined in the academic literature. That kind may be far too grand a thing to be realistic, but it is right that it should be attempted.

5.3 Permitting Virtue

A common response to the claim that the criminal law can make people good is to say that the criminal law is about preventing harmful conduct, not "making people moral". In other words, it is about stopping us being little devils, not making us into angels.

Most criminal law textbooks in their opening chapter emphasise the importance to criminal lawyers of the harm principle. In short this states that an activity should not be criminal if it does not cause harm. In particular the law should not criminalise acts which are harmless just because they are seen as immoral. John Mill (1848), seen by some as the architect of the harm principle, wrote:

> The only purpose for which power can be rightfully exercised over any member of a civilized community against his will is to prevent harm to others. His own good, either physical or moral, is not a sufficient warrant. He cannot rightfully be compelled to do or forebear . . . because in the opinion of others to do so would be wise or even right.

Joel Feinberg (1984) put it this way:

> It is always a good reason in support of penal legislation that it would be effective in preventing (eliminating, reducing) harm to persons other than the actor (the one prohibited from acting) and there is no other means that is equally effective at no greater cost to other values.

Under this principle each person should be free to live their life how they wish unless in doing so they unjustifiable harm another. So, although you may be convinced your neighbour is making foolish or even immoral decisions, they should be free to live how they like unless they are harming others. We can see this principle at work in most current legal systems: You would not get very far if you contacted the police and complained that your friend has a terrible dress sense, is wasting their life endlessly watching Netflix, or is not eating an environmentally sensitive diet. These are their choices, they are not (directly) harming others and you would be told to "mind your own business"—if you are lucky. It seems, then, that the harm principle is an important bulwark against any attempt to promote moral behaviour. But in response we would make the following points.

Let us take the example of omissions. English criminal law does not generally punish omissions. As is well known, a person who walks on past a drowning child, offering no rescue because they do not want to damage their shoes, is not liable for any criminal offence, unless it can be shown that there is a particular duty of care. The *criminal* law only imposes such onerous duties in very special circumstances—such as where the defendant is a doctor (and hence owes a duty to a patient) or a parent (and hence owes a duty to their child). Where such a special duty exists, and a reasonable person in the defendant's position has been breached, and the breach has resulted in harm, the defendant will be criminally liable.

This, we think, is appropriate for a state seeking to make people good. As Madden Dempsey and Herring (2009) put it, the disadvantage of criminalisation is that "it often establishes an authority relationship between the state and its subjects, whereby the subjects repeatedly obey the authority's directives". The problem with that is that "repeated obedience to authority . . .tends to weaken one's rational capacities". In other words where an act is made criminal citizens need to make little effort in assessing what is morally the correct thing to do, absent some overwhelming reasons they obey the law. Where, therefore, in general people do the right thing, using their own moral judgement, then something is lost by requiring them to do the right thing. What is lost is that people are deprived of the (moralising and humanising requirement) to exercise moral judgement and act for good reasons. A practical example: if in a particular society people dutifully picked up their litter because they appreciated the environmental and social benefit of doing so, it would not be appropriate to make not picking up litter unlawful—because then people would start picking up litter to avoid a fine, rather than for their good reasons. As Joseph Raz (1986) has explained, authority is normally justified if it means that a citizen is more likely to comply with right reasons 'if he accepts the directive. . .as authoritatively finding, and tries to follow [it], than if he tries to follow the reasons which apply to him directly."

This argument seems particularly pertinent in relations to the law on commissions. If it is correct (and evidence would suggest it is (Dressler 2000)) that the criminalisation of omissions does not have an impact on whether people do in fact rescue those in peril, then criminalisation is not justifiable. It would deprive those who currently rescue out of bravery, love or concern for their fellow human being, to opportunity to act for those motives, without increasing the number of those who rescued.

5.4 Acts The State Must Criminalize

It is commonly said that criminalisation should be seen as a last resort because it impacts on citizens' freedoms. It is justified only in the name of preserving the autonomy of others. Joseph Raz (1986, p. 418) argues:

> A moral theory which values autonomy highly can justify restricting the autonomy of one person for the sake of the greater autonomy of others or even of that person himself in the future. That is why it can justify coercion to prevent harm, for harm interferes with autonomy. But it will not tolerate coercion for other reasons. The availability of repugnant options, and even their free pursuit by individuals, does not detract from their autonomy. Undesirable as those conditions are they may not be curbed by coercion.

This is a very negative and rather weak justification for criminalisation. Criminal law plays an important role in providing structures and shape to society, and opening up the possibility of individual and societal goods that are far more valuable than mere autonomy. Peter Cane (2006, p. 21) argues:

> Human beings are individuals, and being able to express that individuality in one's choices and actions is an essential component of human well-being. Alongside the individuality of human beings, however, their other most noticeable characteristic is sociability. It is not just that most people choose to live in (larger or smaller) communities or that most people belong to various overlapping and interacting groups. People are also heavily reliant on those communities and groups, and on their relationships with other human beings. If individual freedom is a precondition of human flourishing so, too is membership of communities and groups, and a rich network of social interactions. Indeed, not only is individual freedom of choice and action of greatest value in social contexts; it seems that it would have little value in any other context. Value is a function of scarcity. Just as time would have little or no value if human beings were immortal, so individual freedom would have little or no value in the absence of external constraints. In this light, it seems hard to justify giving the individual's interest in freedom of choice lexical priority over the interest in social cooperation and coordination.

Many of the things that are most valuable need the protection of the criminal law if they are to be enjoyed freely. If there were no law of sexual offences, entering sexual relationships would be fraught with danger; with no law on domestic abuse, moving in with a partner would be risky; with no criminal law regulating doctors, seeking medical advice would be dangerous. And in all of these examples women would be particularly at risk. Of course, the existence of the criminal law does not mean there is not abuse in these or other settings; nor is it true that without the criminal law there would be constant abuse. However, with the deterrent value of the criminal law the state is doing what it can to make these potentially risky activities, in which much good can be done, safer. And note that the criminal law facilitates not only mere autonomy (important though that is) but also the flourishing of love, care and nurturing.

The European Court of Human Rights has held that the European Convention on Human Rights not only restricts the actions of the state but also imposes positive obligations (*Islam (AP) v Secretary of State for the Home Dept* [1999] 2 All ER 545). So article 3, which protects the right to be free from torture and inhuman and degrading treatment, requires that the state not only avoids such activities, but also has in place an effective set of laws which protect individuals from that harm. This is an understandable stance for the court to take. A right to protection from torture or inhuman or degrading treatment would be weak if it meant only that individuals had the right not to suffer that conduct at the hands of the state. Hence in *A v UK* [1998] 3 FCR 557 the British law which failed to make it an offence for a defendant to administer 'reasonable chastisement' to his child was held to have failed to protect the child's rights under article 3. There is a particular obligation on the state to protect the article 3 rights of vulnerable people, such as children. The state is, therefore, obliged to put in place civil and criminal laws to protect people from conduct which infringes their rights under article 3 and there should be adequate enforcement of those laws and appropriate investigation of alleged breaches.

A similar analysis is used in relation to article 8, which protects the right to a person's private and family life, his or her home and correspondence. Within the right to respect for private life is the right to bodily integrity. But there is more to it than this. The right to private life includes the right to 'psychological integrity . . . a right to personal development, and the right to establish and develop relationships with other human beings and the outside world' (*Pretty v UK* (2002) 35 EHRR 1). As with article 3 this has been interpreted to mean not only that the state must not interfere with article 8 rights, but must also protect an individual's article 8 rights. However, in this case article 8(2) sets out circumstances in which an individual's rights can be interfered with. So the state can be justified in failing to provide adequate protection through the law from infringements within a person's article 8 rights, if that failure could be justified under article 8(2).

A good example of how these principles operate is *MC v Bulgaria* (no. 39272/98). In that case a woman complained that the Bulgarian law of rape and the investigation of an alleged sexual assault on her infringed her rights under the ECHR. The court agreed that there were positive obligations on the state to ensure that individuals were protected from acts by other individuals which breached 'fundamental values and essential aspects of private life' (para 150). This positive obligation included the enactment of law proscribing 'grave acts such as rape' and adequate investigation and prosecution of those offences. The court was reluctant to be prescriptive over the exact nature of the offences required, stating:

> . . . [i]n respect of the means to ensure adequate protection against rape States undoubtedly enjoy a wide margin of appreciation. In particular, perceptions of a cultural nature, local circumstances and traditional approaches are to be taken into account. (para 154)

Nevertheless the court went on to find that a requirement of physical resistance by the victim in order for an offence to be committed was inadequate. They added:

> . . . member States' positive obligations under Articles 3 and 8 of the Convention must be seen as requiring the penalization and effective prosecution of any non-consensual sexual act, including in the absence of physical resistance by the victim. (para 166)

It is important to appreciate that the obligation on the state is to ensure that the legal system offers protection to the victim or potential victim from having their rights interfered with. This does not necessarily require the use of the criminal law. In a concurring judgment Judge Tulkens emphasized that the states should not assume that the criminal law was the most effective way of dealing with harmful conduct, and indeed that criminal law should be a last resort. Indeed in some circumstances civil law may offer a victim in danger a more effective protection (e.g. in a case involving child protection issues). Removal of a child from abusive parents is better done through the civil law than the criminal law, for example. In less dramatic cases it may be that civil or other interventionist measures will be as effective a deterrent and hence as effective a way of protecting the rights of the victims. However, it should be remembered that individuals have an absolute right to protection from having their article 3 rights infringed. So if the criminal law is the most effective way of protecting their rights, any less effective protection may not be justifiable. This should be contrasted with article 8 rights, which can be interfered with in the circumstances listed in paragraph 2. Here the use of the criminal law to protect one party's article 8 rights might interfere with the rights of others (e.g. potential defendants) to such an extent as to make it unjustifiable to use the criminal law.

5.5 Conclusion

This chapter has argued that there is much more for the criminal law to do in the enterprise of making people good than simply stopping them doing bad things. First, through the criminal justice system the state is able to express its censure of the defendant's behaviour and embark on a moral conversation with the defendant, designed to restore the defendant to the fold of the moral community. As Liat Levanon (2019, p. 65) argues:

> Positive censure therefore works to mend that which has been torn or broken by the wrongdoing. It engages the wrongdoer in a constructive process, communicates with potential wrongdoers, restores social values, and re-establishes mutual recognition between the wrongdoer and the authority.

The criminal law also helps to create a moral society—a society where particular kinds of wrongful and harmful acts to others are publicly acknowledged and decried. Second, it has been argued that the limits of the criminal law show that the law encourages citizens to display their own virtue through good acts which are not compelled by the state. And third, it is argued that the criminal law provides a structure within which citizens are free to engage safely, or at least more safely, in morally good acts of care, love and nurture.

References

Bennett C (2019) How should we argue for a censure theory of punishment. In: du Bois-Pedain A, Bottoms A (eds) Penal censure: engagements within and beyond desert theory. Hart Publishing, Oxford, pp 109–140

Bogg A, Herring J (2010) Addiction and responsibility. In: Herring J, Regan C, Weinberg D, Withington P (eds) Intoxication: problematic pleasures. Routledge, Abingdon

Bottoms AE (2019) Penal censure, repentance and desistance. In: du Bois-Pedain A, Bottoms A (eds) Penal censure: engagements within and beyond desert theory. Hart Publishing, Oxford, pp 109–140

Cane P (2006) Taking law seriously: starting points of the Hart/Devlin debate. J Ethics 10:21–51

Canton R (2019) Censure, dialogue and reconciliation. In: du Bois-Pedain A, Bottoms A (eds) Penal censure: engagements within and beyond desert theory. Hart Publishing, Oxford, pp 253–274
Crown Prosecution Service (2018) Code for criminal prosecutors. CPS, London
Dressler J (2000) Some brief thoughts (mostly negative) about "Bad Samaritan" laws. Santa Clara Law Rev 40:971–1001
du Bois-Pedain A (2017) Punishment as an inclusionary practice: sentencing in a liberal constitutional state. In: du Bois-Pedain A (ed) Criminal law and the authority of the state. Hart, Oxford
Duff RA (2001) Punishment, communication and community. Oxford University Press, Oxford
Duff RA (2007) Answering for crime. Cambridge University Press, Cambridge
Duff RA (2018) The realm of the criminal law. Oxford University Press, Oxford
Duff RA, Marshall S (1998) Criminalization and sharing wrongs. Can J Law Jurisprud 11(1):7–22
Feinberg J (1984) The moral limits of criminal law. Oxford University Press, Oxford
Gardner J (2007) Offences and defences. Oxford University Press, Oxford
Gross H (2012) Crime and punishment: a concise moral critique. Oxford University Press, Oxford
Lamond G (2007) What is a crime? Oxf J Leg Stud 27:609–619
Lee Y (2015) Can criminal law do without moralism?, Review of crime and punishment: a concise moral critique by Hyman Gross. J Moral Philos 12:103–112
Levanon L (2019) Reflective censure: punishment and human development. In: du Bois-Pedain A, Bottoms A (eds) Penal censure: engagements within and beyond desert theory. Hart Publishing, Oxford, pp 41–66
Madden Dempsey M (2011) Public wrongs and the 'criminal law's business': when victims won't share. In: Cruft R, Kramer M, Reiff M (eds) Crime, punishment and responsibility. Oxford University Press, Oxford, pp 254–272
Madden Dempsey M, Herring J (2009) Rethinking the criminal law's response to sexual offences: on theory and context. In: McGlynn C, Munro V (eds) Rethinking rape law. Routledge, Abingdon
Maslen H (2017) Remorse, penal theory and sentencing. Hart, Oxford
Mill JS (1848) On liberty. John Parker & Son, West Strand, London
Raz J (1986) The morality of freedom. Clarendon Press, Oxford
Tasioulas J (2006) Punishment and repentance. Philosophy 81:279–299
Von Hirsch A (1996) Censure and sanctions. Oxford University Press, Oxford

Chapter 6
Medical Law

Abstract It might be thought that medical law is an area where the law would be particularly apt at promoting good behaviour. In fact, medical law has largely developed by adopting principles from other areas of the law, such as tort and criminal law. This chapter argues that a more ethically robust approach to medical law could be developed if a more sophisticated version of what humans are were developed. A version based on human vulnerability and the interconnectedness of humans would be an excellent starting point.

Keywords Confidentiality · Organ donation · End of life · Abortion · Consent

6.1 Introduction

The term 'medical law' covers a vast legal territory, including liability in tort and sometimes contract where a clinician has not come up to the standard expected, liability in tort and crime for providing treatment without adequate consent, criminal liability for gross negligence manslaughter and medical murder, euthanasia (which, in England, *is* murder) and assisted suicide, breach of the obligation of confidentiality, the provision, withholding and withdrawal of treatment from patients who cannot make their own decisions, abortion, assisted reproduction, the use of body parts—including organ donation, and the definition of death. In short, all human life from before birth to after death.

There is inevitably a strong ethical flavour to many of the questions discussed by medical lawyers, and being able to distinguish carefully between legal and ethical questions is a crucial basic skill.

We cannot possibly do proper justice to even one of the many interfaces between medical law and personal morality, and we do not try. What follows is a brief survey of medical law, starting before birth and ending after death, with some comments about the moral presumptions embodied in each area of the law, and about whether (and if so how) the law should attempt to influence personal morality in each of those areas.

© The Author(s), under exclusive license to Springer Nature Switzerland AG 2021
C. Foster, J. Herring, *The Law as a Moral Agent*, SpringerBriefs in Law,
https://doi.org/10.1007/978-3-030-71334-8_6

6.2 Abortion and the Status of the Embryo/Fetus

It is unfortunate that judicial and legislative consideration of the status of the embryo and fetus has largely been in the context of the law of abortion, and hence largely in terms of a perceived competition between the embryo/fetus and the mother. The law appears to have adopted and to be ruled by Judith Jarvis Thompson's famous thought experiment of the violinist vitally connected for nine months to an unrelated adult, using that other adult as a life-support machine. To question the perfection and applicability of this analogy with abortion is often to be seen as reactionary and paternalistic. We do not enter the debate, save to observe that anything as complex as the relationship between a mother and her unborn child is unlikely to be captured completely satisfactorily by a single imagined scenario. Thomson has some valuable points to make, but there are others too.

The legal upshot has been that the embryo/fetus is for most purposes invisible to the law until it emerges from and is no longer dependent on the mother. The Offences Against The Person Act 1861, section 58 is one of the few places where there is explicit recognition of some sort of legal status of the embryo/fetus. But this is a very limited acknowledgment: a person who performs an abortion is liable to prosecution under the section unless it has been performed in accordance with the Abortion Act 1967 as amended—a decriminalising statute which has decriminalised (or at least led to the non-prosecution of) the vast majority of abortions in England. The broad position in England, then, is that articulated in the Strasbourg case of *Vo v France* (2005) 49 EHHR 12, in which the majority held that until a child emerged from its mother's body it was not automatically regarded as a member of the class of *'toutes personnes'* whose right to life was guaranteed by Article 2 of the ECHR. Thus Lord Mustill in *A-G's Reference (No. 3 of 1994)* [1998] AC 245, 261 could summarise the status of the unborn child as follows: '[I]t is established beyond doubt for the criminal law, as for the civil law. . . .that the child en ventre sa mere does not have a distinct human personality, whose extinguishment gives rise to any penalties or liabilities at common law.'

As soon as a child is born, it has all the protection the law gives to anyone. A born child is conclusively deemed to be a blessing of a magnitude that cancels out any financial or other detriment. Thus where a child is born as a result of clinical negligence (e.g. by reason of a failed sterilisation operation), there can be no claim for the upkeep of that child, although the relevant duty was precisely a duty to prevent the birth of a child: see *Macfarlane v Tayside Health Board* [1999] UKHL 50. Although the time limits enshrined in the Abortion Act were originally fixed on the basis of the fetus's assumed ability to survive independently at a particular stage of gestation, except in the terms of the Abortion Act the criterion of survivability plays no part in determining the protection given by the law to the developing fetus: as *Vo* showed, there is no incremental accrual of rights with increasing gestational age. Birth is the crucial watershed: potential survivability assuming birth at a particular gestational age is not a watershed at all. For a fetus with a significant disability, abortion to term is legally possible—a fact that is hard logically or morally to square with the policy considerations expressed in Macfarlane (and which extend even to disabled children), unless the geographical situation of the fetus (within or outside the mother) is deemed to be a consideration so decisive that it should trump all other considerations. Even if it should trump all other considerations where the mother would otherwise face (as per the Judith Jarvis Thomson metaphor) months of bitterly resented parasitic inhabitation, it is not necessarily obvious that it should trump all other considerations (and particularly the Macfarlane-type considerations) when the period of inhabitation is very short.

It is not easy, either, to square the anxious and respectful consideration given to the embryo by the Human Fertilisation and Embryology Authority ('HFEA': the body to whom decisions in relation to the creation, retention, and use of early embryos are statutorily delegated) with the remarkably simple analysis of the (non) protection of the embryo/fetus when developing inside a uterus.

Judges have frequently said that the embryo/fetus has *some* moral status. In St George's NHS Trust v S for instance, Judge LJ noted that 'Whatever else it may be, a 36 week foetus is not nothing; if viable, it is not lifeless, and it is certainly human.' ([1998] 3 All R 673, at 687). The Polkinghorne Committee, which examined the use of foetuses and fatal material in research, contended for 'a special status for the living human foetus at every stage of its development which we wish to characterise as a profound respect based on its potential to develop into a fully formed human being.' (Polkinghorne 1989).

But little, outside the deliberations of the HFEA—deliberations in very specific and technologically specific contexts—seems to be done with that moral status. It almost always gives way to the wishes of the mother. We make no moral judgment about that legal fact here: we simply record it. But perhaps there is some merit in the old adage that good ethics (and by extension good law) demands good facts. If the fact is (as it is) that the biology of the fetus changes dramatically over the nine months of gestation so that, by the end, it is materially identical with the biology of a child at term, there needs to be a compelling reason why it should be treated as legally identical with a one day embryo. Is maternal autonomy a sufficiently compelling reason? We ask the question, and do not supply the answer.

If the law of abortion, as it works in England, is ethically right, then maternal autonomy is supreme. Some general criticisms of the supremacy of autonomy should arguably apply to the way that autonomy operates in the domain of abortion. We do not enlarge on those general criticisms here.

Abortion, for the overwhelming majority of women, is not undertaken lightly. It is often the cause of great soul-searching and distress. It is generally seen by women as morally serious. Were this not the case, we might advocate making abortion more legally difficult than it is, with a view to underlining the moral status of the fetus—for respect for the moral status of the fetus is connected inextricably to respect for the moral status of all humans. We cannot support such increased stringency on those grounds. But it does not follow that we endorse the status quo. On the contrary, there is a casualness in the *system* which does tend to devalue human life per se. An example is the alleged pre-signing by doctors of the necessary authorisation—indicating prejudgement of the application of the criteria for abortion. Another is the fact that in relation to the requirement to warn about the risks and complications of medical and surgical procedures, the law of abortion seems—on the basis of no discernible legal principles at all, to be immune to the rigour of the usual rules. We are troubled, too, by the capacity to abort to term on the basis of fetal disability. This ability has been much criticised by disability advocates who contend that the attitude to disabilities of all kinds evinced by this ability is widely and deeply repercussive: it tends to callousness. We can see no convincing answer to their arguments.

6.3 Clinical Negligence

We have already outlined (in Chap. 3, on the law of tort), the elements of a negligence claim, and highlight here only the use of the *Bolam* test, as interpreted by *Bolitho* (which is explained in Chap. 3). Its use now is constrained tightly by the hegemony of clinical guidelines, which increasingly enshrine evidence-based practice. If the scientific literature conclusively demonstrates that practice A (which is financially comparable to practice B) produces better results than practice B, it cannot be coherently argued that there is a *responsible* body of opinion in the relevant speciality which would adopt practice A. The *Bolam* test does not cease to be the principle determining both the standard of care and the way of proving that the standard has been discharged, but the presence of an authoritative guideline makes the answers to the questions posed by *Bolam* obvious.

The *Bolam/Bolitho* test, by making *responsible* practice its touchstone, discourages mavericks while seeking not to discourage innovation. In most clinical contexts the connection with personal morality is not obvious, though the test may have the effect of reining in (for the moral good of the individual practitioners and the medical good of their patients) some more unreflectively paternalistic practitioners. This effect is most obvious in clinical negligence cases involving allegedly inadequate counselling/taking of consent.

The importance of respecting and facilitating patient choice has increasingly been recognised. The House of Lords case of *Sidaway v Royal Bethlem Hospital* [1985] AC 871, in which the different contributing Law Lords articulated very different ways of seeing the duty owed to patients in the context of the consenting process, was interpreted, for a while, as vindicating the simple application of the *Bolam* test to that process: the law would expect the process to be conducted in a way that would be endorsed by a responsible body of relevant opinion.

But that changed. Incrementally, over the following quarter of a century, the more patient-centred approach to consenting that had been advocated by Lord Scarman in *Sidaway* began to take centre stage. This was the 'prudent patient' approach (adopted in some other jurisdictions, for example Australia: e.g. *Rogers v Whittaker* (1992) 175 CLR 479 (High Court of Australia) whereby there was an obligation to reveal a risk of which a prudent patient would wish to know. The central importance of respecting patient autonomy was finally acknowledged by the UK Supreme Court in *Montgomery v Lanarkshire Health Board* [2015] UKSC 11, paragraph 87. The court said:

> The doctor is therefore under a duty to take reasonable care to ensure that the patient is aware of any material risks involved in any recommended treatment, and of any reasonable alternative or variant treatments.

The test of materiality is whether, in the circumstances of the particular case, a reasonable person in the patient's position would be likely to attach significance to the risk, or the doctor is *or should reasonably be aware* that the particular patient would be likely to attach significance to it.' (Para 87, emphasis added).

It will be clear from the parts in italics in the citation above that (despite the way that *Montgomery* has been widely represented) *Bolam* has not been banished from the law of consent. Far from it. It continues to contribute crucially to the determination of what it is reasonable to expect a doctor to do in ensuring that a patient is aware of risks, of what 'reasonable alternative or variant treatments' are, and whether it is reasonable to expect a doctor to be aware that a particular patient would be likely to attach significance to a particular risk. And indeed it will be rare that a reasonable patient would be likely to attach significance to a risk when a reasonable doctor would not.

The formal legal effect of *Montgomery,* then, has been massively overstated. But that overstatement itself has produced a significant change in medical culture. It has dealt a body blow to medical paternalism, and put patients at the centre of the decision-making process. Perhaps (it is early days) the effect has not been all good. It may encourage a consumerist culture in medicine, with doctors seen not as professionals but as the providers of a product. It may mean that clinicians spend on a pointless box-ticking exercise time that would be better spent on other aspects of patient care. It may mean that patients are told about risks they would rather not know about, causing unnecessary distress. But it is not fanciful to hope that the overall effect will be to encourage clinicians to see patients as individuals, embedded in a social context which will modify the risks that are perceived to be relevant, and that this itself will lead to more personal, compassionate, holistic and, generally, moral care. It may dilute the reductionist tendency to treat not patients but clinical problems. If that proves to be the case, *Montgomery* will be a clear example of an instance of the law evolving in a way that promotes individual morality, in a context where it is clearly appropriate to do so.

What is perhaps least morally satisfactory about the ethos of clinical negligence litigation is the limited view that it has of the responsibilities of clinicians. A duty is generally owed to a patient—and 'patient' is generally construed very narrowly. The general policy reasons for this limitation have been discussed in the chapter on the law of tort. But there are surely reasons in a clinical context to widen the categories of potential claimant. Certainly patients are more likely than non-patients to be affected by a tortious act or default, but many non-patients are entirely foreseeably affected too. If a psychiatrist negligently discharges a homicidal patient into the community, it is foreseeable that *someone* will be killed or hurt. If a patient is negligently not warned about the risk of recanalization of the vas deferens after vasectomy, and so does not attend for the post-operative examination which would have demonstrated the presence of sperm in his semen, it is foreseeable that a non-patient who does not want to become pregnant may do so—even if that non-patient can only be identified as the member of a large and unascertainable class (namely those with whom the patient might have unprotected sexual intercourse). Is it really not fair, just, and reasonable to say that the doctor owes a duty to these foreseeably affected claimants? Would it really open the floodgates, distorting the insurance market in a way so deleterious to wider society that it is better to keep the potential claimants out of a remedy than to risk the market distortion?

In the realm of clinical negligence, as elsewhere in the law of tort, the law has been very cautious about extending the ambit of a clinician's duty. There is one recent English case which indicates that the law might be realising that it is not satisfactory to see the patient as a discrete entity, unconnected to others. This is the case of *ABC v St. George's Healthcare NHS Trust and others* [2017] EWCA Civ 336; [2020] EWHC 455 (QB). A patient of the defendant NHS Trust had Huntingdon's disease. This meant that his daughter, who was pregnant at the material time, had a 50% chance of having the disease (and if she did, her fetus had a 50% chance of being affected). The father refused to allow the clinicians to tell the daughter of his diagnosis (and hence alert her to the risk of her/her fetus being affected). The default position would conventionally be that the clinicians should not breach the duty of confidentiality owed to the father (as we will see in the Confidentiality section below). But was it not different here? Should the daughter not be regarded as a patient to whom a duty was owed? Should not, indeed, genetic information (which by its very nature is shared with others) be seen as being held in a joint-account with others. The Court of Appeal said that, in principle, a duty might be owed to the daughter, and when the case was subsequently tried the trial judge decided that the father's clinicians owed a duty to balance his interests in non-disclosure against the daughter's interests in disclosure.

It remains to be seen what effect this judgment has on the wider law of clinical negligence: will it, of instance, be restricted to cases of genetic counselling (we can see no justification for such a restriction—and the trial judge agreed). But its primary significance for this book is that it is a recognition that humans are not islands: that the duties which are owed to them by others may arise because of the relationship that the potential claimant has with another: indeed that all duties have to be seen as duties owed to entities who are, as a matter of definition, quintessentially *relational* entities. This acknowledgment has enormous corollaries for personal morality. For if we are the beneficiary of a wider duty, arising out of the fact of our relationality, it surely follows that we should act towards others in a way that reflects our relational nature. It will no longer do to behave in our private lives in accordance with the law's old pastiche of human nature—the pastiche that says that we are entirely self-determining and owe nothing to anyone or anyone else. The decision in *ABC* goes some way towards aligning the law with the anthropological, biological, and sociological fact (a fact with momentous ethical consequences) that we are porous creatures who bleed into one another.

6.4 Consent Generally

In relation to capacitous patients, there is a near-absolute right to decide what is done to one's body. In most decisions made about her own body, the patient is supreme: as long as she does not harm others and otherwise obeys the general law, there is little she is required to do and little she need refrain from doing. The law, in other words, sees her as an island—a view with ethical consequences that we have already criticised. We would not, however, have the default position otherwise: the ability to make a morally good choice obviously presumes the ability to make a choice that is not morally good. That is not to say that we think that restraints on personal action can never be justified on moral grounds. Of course they can, and indeed much of this book is devoted to discussing when such restraints are appropriate. But in relation to what one can do with one's own body, when such use does not harm others we agree, generally, with the principle of self-sovereignty.

There are some important qualifications to the basic principle. The main qualification is in respect of significant bodily injury. Thus one cannot validly consent to significant bodily injury that has no therapeutic purpose (many forms of surgery will amount to such injury, but generally they are done with a view to improving the patient's condition). Sado-masochistic practices involving serious injury to, inter alia, the genitalia were declared by a majority of the House of Lords to be unlawful—essentially on public policy grounds (*R v Brown* [1983] UKHL 19; *Laskey et al v UK* (1997) 24 EHRR 39). Arguments under the European Convention on Human Rights (ECHR) featured in that case: they would feature much more prominently now. The main ruling provision of the ECHR is Article 8. It is a very elastic article which has expanded in the hands of the Strasbourg court to cover many situations that could not have been envisaged by its draftsman. It is the main ECHR provision under which notions of human autonomy and dignity operate, and which governs the general relationship between our individual aspirations to live our lives as we choose, and the obligations and restrictions which result from our membership of society. The article reads:

1. Everyone has the right to respect for his private and family life, his home and his correspondence.
2. There shall be no interference by a public authority for the exercise of this right except such as is in accordance with the law and is necessary in a democratic society in the interests of natural security, public safety or the economic well-being of the country, for the prevention of disorder or crime, for the protection of health or morals, or for the protection of the rights and freedoms of others.

Article 8(1) protects an individual's right. Article 8(2) allows the individual's right to be curtailed in the interests of the society of which that individual is a part. The tension between 8(1) and 8(2) is the tension that characterises citizenship.

The jurisprudence on Article 8 is voluminous and complex. Most of it is concerned with how to strike the balance between the demands of 8(1) and the considerations of 8(2). Examination of individual decisions sheds little light on the questions with which we are concerned here. *R v Brown* (the sado-masochism case mentioned above) might well be decided differently today. There are difficult and complex questions about, for instance, cosmetic surgery, tongue-splitting, body-piercing, contact sports and other dangerous sports, and so on. The important point for present purposes is that Article 8 recognises (as the genetic counselling case of *ABC* did) that as an ontological fact humans do not stand alone—from which it follows that the law should not act as if they do.

The position about patients lacking capacity is more complex. If a patient cannot make a decision for herself, a decision made on her behalf will be lawful if it is made in her best interests. In deciding what is in a patient's best interests a number of criteria must be considered. They are set out in s. 4 of the Mental Capacity Act 2005. They are all directed towards respecting the patient's autonomy. The patient should be encouraged to participate in the process insofar as she can, her past and present wishes and feelings should be considered, and in relation to assessing what would amount to a decision which the patient, if autonomous, would have made for herself, soundings should be taken from those who know the patient and can speak to those issues.

The s. 4 criteria all relate to the best interests of the patient herself—not to the interests of anyone else. They may seem, therefore, to embody and perpetuate the idea that humans are not necessarily relational creatures. And that, given the autonomistic focus of the 2005 Act, is no doubt how it was envisaged the best interests test would work. But it need not necessarily do so. Capacitous people often choose, autonomously, to be altruistic or otherwise act in a way that acknowledges their non-atomistic nature. If the purpose of the best interests test is to facilitate decisions that would have been made if the patient had capacity, why should altruistic decisions not be endorsed by the Act?

Considerations similar to those under the Act apply to decisions made on behalf of children. We do not deal here with the legal mechanics, in England, of making such decisions, and say simply that we acknowledge that it is more ethically problematic to endorse altruism—and particularly damaging altruism—on the part of a child who legally lacks capacity. This is because the child is unlikely to have a sufficiently well-evidenced track record of altruism, and because, if cognitively capacitous, may be unable properly to balance the benefits (which may be subtle) and harms of altruism. Legally supportable decisions in relation to children therefore tend to be based on a narrow construction of best interests: best interests are commonly seen as identical with 'medical' best interests, despite judicial reminders that a more holistic audit of best interests is required.

Sometimes strenuous efforts are made to characterise as 'best interests' a decision that the child herself would not have made because it is clearly the right thing to do. A good example is where a bone marrow transplant needs to be taken from a child, (whom we will call X), in order to save the life of her sibling, Y. A bone marrow transplant is painful and traumatic. If X refuses to comply, can it be said that it is in her best interests to be restrained and the bone marrow forcibly taken? It can, and it commonly is. It tends to be held that, if the bone marrow is not taken, and Y dies, Y's death will affect X far more profoundly than the taking of the bone marrow. A capacitous adult in X's position would probably consent to the bone marrow being taken. This might be altruism: it might be self-interest (the adult might know, for example, how they would be affected by their sibling's death, or how others would feel about them if they knew that donation might have been life-saving but had nonetheless been refused). A child (often) cannot be credited with the foresight and knowledge of the world upon which that sort of reasoning depends, and so must be given the benefit of the decision-maker's greater experience. While this sort of reasoning sounds plausible, it is hard not to think that the real reason for the approval of the compulsory extraction of bone marrow is simply the fact that it is a morally good thing to try to save a sibling. We do not quibble with the use of the best interests to achieve that result. It is an example of the law encouraging action that, if it had the mind-set to go with it, would be altruism, and an example of the law acknowledging our porous, relational nature.

6.5 Confidentiality

However much we see ourselves as communitarian beings, the right to secrets is generally regarded as important. And so, in most cultures, there is a concomitant ethical and legal prohibition on divulging secrets without permission. Jewish law, for instance, concludes that express permission is needed to pass on anything at all about another. In the Torah one often sees specific instructions to say something. Moses, for instance, might be told 'Say to the Children of Israel. . . .'. These injunctions are so regular as to be strange. Why are they needed? The answer, says Jewish law, is that without a specific dispensation Moses would be committing a sin by relating anything that God had said to him. As for God and Moses, so for us and everyone else. Jewish law recognises that there are some circumstances when confidences can and indeed should be breached—notably when to keep a secret would cause serious harm, and, sometimes when, absent the disclosure, someone might enter a damaging relationship. But secrecy remains the default position. Secret-keeping, here, is *ethically* important. To divulge a secret not only causes or might cause harm to the person to whom the secret relates: it is also a moral wrong—a theme taken up in the New Testament by Jesus: we are defiled not by what goes into our mouths, but by what comes out (Matthew 15: 11).

If it is right that secret-breaking is, generally, a wrong, then, as we have already noted in the crime and tort chapters, laws that will tend to discourage that wrong-doing are likely to be morality-promoting.

If a particular action or inaction is wrong, and our ethical sensitivities are properly adjusted, then our consciences are likely to tell us. And indeed, in the realm of confidentiality, conscience has sometimes been used explicitly as a legal benchmark. Thus in *R v Department of Health ex p Source Informatics [1999] EWCA Civ 3011*, which concerned the supply of information by pharmacists to data collection companies, Simon Brown LJ, having reviewed the authorities, said:

> To my mind the one clear and consistent theme emerging from all these authorities is this the confidant is placed under a duty of good faith to the confider and the touchstone by which to judge the scope of his duty and whether or not it has been fulfilled or breached is his own conscience, no more and no less. One asks, therefore, on the facts of this case: would a reasonable pharmacist's conscience be troubled by the proposed use to be made of patients' prescriptions? Would he think that by entering [the data collection agency's] scheme he was breaking his customers' confidence, making unconscientious use of the information they provide?. . . . (para 31)

There are problems with this formulation: its reference to the 'reasonable pharmacist' is uncomfortably reminiscent of the *Bolam* test. The *Bolam* test can be defended when it purports to determine liability in matters that are the subject of the exercise of technical clinical judgment or other skill, but where the subject matter of the dispute is straightforwardly ethical (as reference to conscience declares the issue of disclosure to be) the justification for its deployment falls away. Nonetheless, as a piece of ethical policing (as opposed to supportable legal reasoning) it is exemplary.

Legal disputes about confidentiality tend instead to be seen as tugs of war between the public interest in disclosure and the public interest in non-disclosure: see *W v Egdell* [1990] 1 Ch 349 and *X v Y and others* [1988] 2 All ER 648. The fact that both of the competing interests are identified as 'public' conduces to the communitarian view of the self that we have repeatedly endorsed. There may be a move away from this analysis, though (at least where the alleged breach is by a public authority), for questions of confidentiality are increasingly viewed through the lens of Article 8 ECHR. The right conferred by Article 8(1) would seem to be private, not public, in nature. It is balanced against the wider societal considerations in 8(2). It seems unlikely that an Article 8 analysis is likely to differ in practice from an analysis under the older law of *W v Egdell,* and of course the whole structure of Article 8 emphasises that individuals are crucially, definingly, socially embedded.

Thus in Jewish law, so in English law: duties of confidentiality, though vital, are not absolute. They give way in situations where the public good demands it (remembering that individuals, for these purposes, as for all purposes, are part of the public). The public good will include the avoidance of serious harm. We recognise the moral potency of the law of confidentiality, and consider that, by and large, it endorses conduct that most would agree should be encouraged. But it is too cautious. In its desire to protect secrets it has often said merely that disclosure of potentially injury-sparing information is permissible rather than mandatory. The law would better reflect and encourage right-speaking and right withholding of speech were it to impose, more often than it does, a positive duty of disclosure. The decision in the genetic counselling case of *ABC,* discussed above, is a tentative step in the right direction. We can see no reason why such duties should be restricted to the context of genetic counselling. There are many reasons for upholding the potential imposition of a duty of disclosure other than the fact that genetic information may be held in a 'joint account'.

6.6 The End of Life

All jurisdictions condemn murder and other forms of homicides. While suicide has been widely decriminalized, most jurisdictions have some sort of restriction on assisting the suicide of another, and on killing another at that other's request. Many jurisdictions, however, see a real moral and legal distinction between active killing or assistance in killing, and the withdrawal or withholding of life-sustaining treatment. The distinction between acts and omissions, therefore, plays an important part in the law of end of life decision-making. When the clinicians responsible for the care of a boy in Permanent Vegetative State (who had to be artificially fed) concluded, with the agreement of his family, that the feeding should be withdrawn, allowing him to die, they were concerned about being charged with murder: see *Airedale NHS Trust v Bland.* [1993] AC 789. They, after all, intended him to die (the *mens rea* of murder), and were responsible for the physical circumstances (the lack of feeding) that would bring about his death. The House of Lords, however, decided that to bring about death in his way would not amount to murder. The decision in *Bland* is a complex one (see Foster 2015 for a full discussion), but central to it was the assertion of the act/omission distinction. Withdrawing life-sustaining food was characterised as an omission: an act is needed for murder.

This is problematic. The act/omission distinction is notoriously elusive. Many powerful thought experiments (for instance some variants of the 'trolley problem') are designed to show that it is illusory. But even if it is not illusory, it does not capture, by itself, the characteristic moral evil of culpable homicide. It is not hard to think of many omissions that are as morally blameworthy as many acts. We consider that the distinction does real moral harm because of its binary simplicity: act = murder: non-act = non-murder. That is not the sort of algorithm that encourages moral reflection, and without moral reflection mere legally compliant behaviour is less moral. It might be said that the real problem lies with the murder/manslaughter dichotomy. Were it to be replaced (the argument would go) with a general substantive offence of homicide with varying degrees of culpability, to be reflected in sentence, the law might more accurately reflect the different moral states associated with killing. Such a reform would mean a more nuanced response to culpability, but if the objective is the inculcation and perpetuation of a particular moral view, that is not necessarily desirable. It may, for instance, be a legitimate function of the law to encourage revulsion for a particular type of behaviour—a revulsion which may mean sentences which are disproportionate to culpability but justified in terms of societal catharsis, or the discouragement of similar offending, or otherwise. In the case of homicide, it may be that the maintenance of respect for the supreme value of human life justifies the dramatic categorisation of deliberate killing as murder (with a mandatory life sentence). One counter-argument would be that if it is life itself that is regarded as particularly sacrosanct (rather than the mental state associated with the taking of life being particularly central) there should be *less* of a distinction between murder and manslaughter—not more.

These arguments, like so many in this book, may turn on empirical evidence (which is sorely lacking) about the way that law affects attitudes.

In relation to assisted suicide and euthanasia, one of the main justifications for the existing English prohibitions (which clearly interfere with the autonomy of some, and may perpetuate the suffering of some) is that they are necessary in order to emphasise and enshrine the notion that human life is valuable. On this view, truncation of autonomy and suffering are prices that have to be paid for the continued enshrinement (and for the protection of vulnerable constituencies and for the prevention of the descent down the slippery slope from voluntary to involuntary euthanasia).

We do not here enter the debate about whether the price is worth paying, but merely suggest that, whatever one thinks of the price, the alternative to such laws would seem inevitably to make such significant concessions to autonomy (which is in a head to head battle with the sanctity of life in this domain) that respect for life is likely to be diluted not just in the courts but also in the minds of individuals.

6.7 Organ Donation

England now has an opt-out system. It remains to be seen whether this increases the supply of organs. The question for us is whether altruism (an attitude and a behaviour which we see as uncontroversially ethical and which we consider the law should strive to encourage) is diminished or enhanced by such a system. That, again, is an empirical question: we can only speculate about the answer. Certainly an opt-in allows a more strenuous declaration of one's altruism than an opt-out system, and it may be that this self-identification as an altruist has the effect of making the person altruistic in areas of their life well away from organ donation. An opt-out system mutes the internal debate about personal altruism, and militates against reflection. That may make us overall less personally moral. Certainly we consider that simple membership of a society that regards it as a high priority to increase the supply of organs has no necessary connotations for the individual: our individual participation in the democratic process is slight.

6.8 Conclusion

Medical law is such a broad discipline that it is impossible to make meaningful generalisations about its ethical objectives or the success of those objectives. We can say, though, that because it tends to be more explicitly concerned with what many would regard as the most fundamental issues of life (birth, sovereignty over one's own body, the end of life, and the disposal of one's body parts after death, for instance), it *should* perhaps be more ethically concerned and literate than many other areas of law. We can see no evidence that it is. Perhaps that is because it has simply borrowed its morality, along with its legal principles, from many other areas—such as crime, tort, family law, and so on. Perhaps it is unreasonable to expect principles so imported to behave more coherently in their new environment than in the place they grew up. Perhaps it is unreasonable not to expect some philosophical dissonance with principles derived from very different areas. But as medical law gradually comes of age, those sorts of excuses sound less convincing. Fundamentally ethical questions demand a systematic approach. That approach, we suggest, must derive from a more sophisticated (and certainly a more explicitly considered) view of what humans are. We won't get our law or our ethics right until we get our anthropology right. We propose that human vulnerability and the interconnectedness of all humans, as the most obvious characteristics of human beings, should be the bulwarks of that anthropology.

References

Foster C (2015) Airedale NHS Trust v Bland [1993]. In: Herring J, Wall J (eds) Landmark cases in medical law. Hart, Oxford

Polkinghorne J (1989) Review of the guidance on the research use of foetuses an foetal material. HMSO, London

Chapter 7
Moral Enhancement

Abstract This chapter considers how the law should respond to technological advances that offer the possibility of moral enhancement. There is little regulation at the moment, but legal intervention will be required as the technologies develop. Without knowing what is scientifically possible it is not possible to state what that regulation should be. But some of the key questions are clear. They include: Does moral bioenhancement threaten individual autonomy by truncating our capacity for agency? Does moral bioenhancement threaten our identity? Will I be less 'me' if I am the subject of these technologies? If some of these fears are or may be real, do the benefits trump any such detriments?

Keywords Enhancement · Morality · Altruism · Disability · Technology

7.1 Introduction

This book has been concerned with the questions of whether the law should seek to make individuals morally better, and if so, how it should do it. Generally, where an intention to improve personal morality can be discerned in the law, it can only be discerned dimly, and usually, where this intention exists, moral improvement is an objective collateral to a more overt one.

But we turn now to deal with technologies whose express purpose is moral improvement. Most are currently speculative, but there are sound scientific grounds for supposing that many such technologies will soon be available.

7.2 Definitions

There is a vast, constantly expanding literature on the ethics of moral enhancement, and we cannot try to do justice to it. For the purpose of this chapter we adopt the two meanings of moral enhancement discussed by Earp et al. (2018), namely: (a) 'Any change in a moral agent, A, effected or facilitated in some significant way by the

© The Author(s), under exclusive license to Springer Nature Switzerland AG 2021

C. Foster, J. Herring, *The Law as a Moral Agent*, SpringerBriefs in Law,
https://doi.org/10.1007/978-3-030-71334-8_7

application of a neurotechnology, that results, or is reasonably expected to result, in A's being a morally better agent.' And (b) a 'beneficial change in moral functioning'. This second sense could be understood in many ways. To define 'beneficial' obviously necessitates making some normative claims. We do not explore here how one would adjudicate such claims, and will concentrate, for the sake of clarity, on changes that are relatively uncontroversially beneficial. But, as Earp et al. point out, to take the discussion further, we must also specify what it is that the intervention seeks to enhance: 'Is it the agent? Her moral character? Her well-being? The function itself?' All but the function itself seems to us to be embodied in meaning (a) (the change in the moral agent), and so we address, as do Earp et al, the function itself, seeing an enhancement as an increase in 'the ability of the function to do what it normally does.'

It is immediately obvious that mere increase in the ability of a function is not necessarily a good thing. To increase the sensitivity of the retina to light might make daylight unbearable. To increase the sensitivity of hearing might make ordinary sounds painful. And so it is with functions associated with morality. Empathy is the most commonly discussed example. Too much empathy might paralyse or contaminate moral decision-making, making it impossible to take into account the interests of anyone or anything other than the object of the empathy. Too much empathy might cause a person to burn out morally—the well-recognised syndrome of 'compassion fatigue'. Only if one thinks that the only moral course of action is to do what one's empathy prompts can one conclude, without any caveat, that to increase empathy will be to increase morality.

All judgments about the propriety of effecting a change in the ability of a morally related function will therefore be crucially context and fact-sensitive.

The distinction between senses (a) and (b) relates clearly to another distinction drawn by Schaefer and endorsed by Earp et al. and others—that between direct moral enhancements (which seek to produce particular behaviour, motives, or ideas) and indirect enhancements (which 'aim at making people more reliably produce the morally correct ideas, motives or behaviours without committing to the content of those ideas, motives and/or actions' (Schaefer 2015, p. 265).

7.3 Arguments for and Against Moral Enhancement

Specker et al. have reviewed the reasons given in the literature for advocating and for deprecating moral bioenhancement (Specker et al. 2014). They identify six broad and overlapping categories of reasons which form the battlegrounds for debate.

These are:

1. *Arguments based on the necessity or non-necessity of moral enhancement* (Wiseman 2014; Harris 2016)

   There are five sub-categories:

(a) *Humans can always improve.*

That means (say the advocates of enhancement) that there are always good reasons for improvement and, depending on the consequences of improvement or non-improvement, there may be a positive duty to improve. Savulescu, arguing on the basis of the morality (and the—for him—concomitant legality) of the duty of safe rescue, would impose a duty to enhance wherever the benefit to the wider community was very great and the detriment to the individual very slight (Savulescu and Persson 2012). As always, we observe, the devil is in the detail. Such declarations are easy to make, but often founder when faced with particularity.

(b) *The biological nature of humans is intrinsically defective*

From which (say the advocates) it follows that their moral evil cannot be cured by education or socialization, and more direct biological interference with their nature is necessary. No, say their opponents: humans are intrinsically good, and even if they are not, it does not follow as a matter of principle that education/socialization are inadequate remedies.

(c) *Traditional remedies are not adequate*

This is the empirical claim that follows from (b) above (Persson and Savulescu 2008).

(d) *Only moral enhancement can avoid major disasters*

Many existential threats are a consequence, according to the advocates, of individual moral failings. If those failings are eliminated or mitigated, we will all be safer. The opponents respond in several ways: perhaps by arguing that not all such threats can be laid at the door of individual morality, or by taking issue with the empirical claim that such failings can be addressed by enhancement technologies.

(e) *The reduction of criminality*

If criminal behaviour can be reduced by moral enhancement, why would one not endorse that use? To which the response might be that a simple equation of non-moral behaviour and criminality is naïve, and that in any event the more general objections to enhancement apply.

2. *Arguments based on the impossibility of sufficient agreement about what enhancement amounts to or entails* (Wiseman 2016)

   There are six sub-categories.

(a) *Do we know sufficient about the mechanics of our moral psychology?*
(b) *Are behavioural changes, absent enhancement, sufficient to address the concerns of the would-be enhancers?*
(c) *Can there be sufficient certainty about the ethical systems to be used in deciding whether or not enhancement is necessary or desirable?*
(d) *Even if there cannot be philosophical certainty, can there be sufficient consensus?*

(e) *Are the situations in which enhancement might be desirable or necessary so fact sensitive that general rules cannot be articulated?*
(f) *Is there a distinction of substance between moral enhancement and the treatment of mental disorders?*

This issue overlaps very considerably with many of the other categories. The question can be asked equally of both the advocates and the opponents of enhancement. If there is no distinction (the proponents would say), what objection can there be to enhancement in a world which accepts that there is such a thing as mental illness, and also that it is ethical to treat it—sometimes compulsorily?

3. *How technically feasible is moral bioenhancement?* (Dubljević and Racine 2017; Dubljević et al. 2020)

There are four sub-categories:

(a) *The current state of scientific knowledge*

Is the necessary knowledge there already, or is more research needed?

(b) *Are limitations imposed by our intrinsic biological complexity or the complexity of our moral psychology?*
(c) *Are there or might there be side effects to the technology which make it unacceptable?*
(d) *Is methodologically and ethically sound research possible?*

4. *Is it possible, ethically, to develop moral enhancement technologies?*

There are two sub-categories:

(a) *Are non-biomedical methods preferable?*

Such methods might include education of various sorts. And is the use of biotechnology 'playing God' in a way that the use of other methods is not?

(b) *Is there a difference in principle between biomedical techniques of enhancement and other techniques?*

Is the important moral debate about the ends rather than the means? If the concern is about the irreversibility of an enhancement, are 'traditional' means any less offensive?

5. *Autonomy, freedom, and identity*

There are three sub-categories:

(a) Does moral bioenhancement threaten individual autonomy, by truncating our capacity for agency? If we *can't* make bad choices, can we be really good? (Harris 2011)
(b) Does moral bioenhancement threaten our identity? Will I be less 'me' if I am the subject of these technologies? (Focquaert and Schermer 2015)
(c) Do the benefits trump any such drawbacks? (Bublitz 2016)

6. *Social effects*

There are five sub-categories (Sandberg and Fabiano 2017):

(a) Moral bioenhancement, unlike most other forms of enhancement, benefits others, and is therefore less morally suspicious.
(b) Moral enhancement might lead to enhanced, and therefore more virtuous, people being exploited. Their altruism, for instance, might be manipulated in a way that is detrimental to them.
(c) Moral enhancement might diminish the moral differences between people in harmful ways. It might, for instance, make only one moral view acceptable, and so create toxic elites.
(d) Enhancement technologies might lead to a dangerous quest for a moral Utopia, in which individual choice may be a casualty.
(e) Moral enhancement may become mandatory. It may, for instance, lead to a demand that parents use technologies to produce the 'best' children they can, with concomitant dangers of discrimination against the non-enhanced, or tyranny by the enhanced or the enhancers.

7.4 A Closer Look at the More Cogent Objections to Enhancement

The most robust (and most discussed) of those objections is that enhancement may change our identity—so amounting to a kind of assassination. X is changed so much that she ceases to be X. Not only does she cease being X, she ceases. She is deceased (Douglas 2008). Behind this objection there is likely to be an appeal to the intrinsic value of naturalness (an appeal vulnerable to the observations above about the desirability, sometimes, of changing the cards dealt out by fate). Suppose, though, that one can identify a case where there is no question of an intervention abating a pathological state. Extreme cognitive enhancement is a good example. X has an IQ of 120. That cannot sensibly be characterized as in any way suboptimal unless 'suboptimal' is defined as any state which does not benefit from every available intervention. Suppose a pill can be taken which, without any side-effects at all, adds 50 IQ points. An IQ of 170 would increase X's valency in many arenas. It would increase his earning capacity, his capacity for practical reasoning (including his ability to perform utilitarian calculations, making him, if one's moral yardstick is utilitarian, a more moral person), and his ability to contribute to the national coffers and to the general well-being of the world. Suppose, too, that he will choose to be a good rather than an evil genius, and that his increased cognitive capacity will increase his own capacity.

There are two reasons why it might nonetheless be ethically inappropriate to allow him to take the pill. The first is founded on the notion of equality—of the level playing field: if he has all the benefits associated with this enhancement, why should others not?

On the facts posited here, equality seems not to be a compelling objection, simply because (as is claimed to be the case for many types of cognitive and moral enhancement) everyone benefits from the enhancement. It is an enhancement of the world. X just happens to be a nerve centre from which the benefits radiate. Should the world be denied the benefits of the enhancements mediated through X because of some slavish worship of the principle of equality? The answer to this last question is 'Possibly'—because to dilute the principle of equality might have toxic fall-out in other areas.

A more worrying objection relates to identity. Adding 50 IQ points might stop X from being himself. It might make X cease to be, and create another entity with an uncertain relationship to X.

The law is generally robustly protective of identity. We have no space here to examine and interrogate the way that the law deals with identity (we have tried to do that elsewhere), but note, for instance, at the deference given to advance directives which enshrine the views of an entity who no longer exists—or whose attributes have changed tectonically. The law's concern there is to mitigate the effect of the assaults by disease or injury on the identity of the pre-morbid patient. A physical or chemical assault which resulted in the loss of the attributes associated with personal identity would be regarded as a particularly terrible crime. An analogy with homicide is not completely fanciful. Many of the reasons given for outlawing the killing of other humans can be framed as reasons for protecting the unique concatenation of attributes collected in one body. And for the same reasons, X's willingness to take the IQ pill might not be a complete answer to the objections based on identity. If the pill stops him being him, it may be as undesirable as suicide. The list of desirable societal benefits that would result from X's enhancement should make us pause to wonder whether X, regardless of whether or not he consents to the enhancement, is being instrumentalized. His altruistic offer to be instrumentalized may be an offer that it is too dangerous to accept. While altruism is generally to be applauded, sometimes it should be discouraged, perhaps to the point of prohibition.

7.5 Are Technological Enhancements Any Different from Non-technological Enhancements?

Much human activity is and has always been about enhancement. We read books in an attempt to understand the world better. We send our children to school. Reading and education more generally produce anatomically demonstrable changes in our brains: they result in more synaptic connections. Before an exam we try to get a good night's sleep—an attempt to maximise the mental processing that occurs during sleep so that our brains function more effectively in the examination. We wake ourselves and keep ourselves awake chemically by drinking coffee. If we're running a long race we'll eat pasta the night before so that glucose is more efficiently available. We watch our diets more generally, hoping that we'll have more effective bodies. We use perfumes to subdue our natural smell and make us more attractive to actual or potential partners. We shave off our hair, or cut it expensively, or wear figure-flattering clothes, for the same reason.

Most of us would see nothing morally questionable about any of these activities. Indeed we might see it as morally dubious not to make strenuous efforts to ensure that our children are educated. And yet many of us are uneasy about other enhancement techniques: for instance administering oxytocin to facilitate bonding with another, or the use of Ritalin to enhance concentration.

Intuitive uneasiness should not be casually ignored. Our intuitions are often the source of insights which are inaccessible to our reason. But intuition, to deserve respect as a valuable moral compass, needs to be consistent. It is hard to see a consistent theme in intuition's objection to enhancement technologies. The objection is plainly not based on the assertion of a distinction between acts and omissions: sending a child to school is an act. So is drinking coffee or shaving. Nor is naturalness obviously the criterion: think about perfumes and coffee—both of which seem to be directed at the *suppression* of naturalness. It might be possible, though, to argue that acceptable enhancements simply modulate what we naturally are, or express or allow us to express more eloquently what we really are. In relation to perfume that would entail saying: 'I know that my natural smell might deter a potential partner. It would prevent me from telling the true story about myself. To use perfume is to remove an objection to me that exists in the mind of another.' We return to this argument below.

Perhaps, though, at least some of the difficulties are artefacts of the way that the debate about human enhancement has been conducted in the Academy. The tendency is to polarize: it makes for more exciting discourse. And so 'enhancement' has been artificially set against 'non-enhancement', without an adequate acknowledgment that much of life entails enhancement, and that the distinction between technological and non-technological enhancement is often elusive and, even when identifiable, of little ethical significance.

7.6 Is Enhancement Really Any Different from Therapy?

We have little moral disagreement with most of medicine. We might sometimes object to over-treatment (for instance working too aggressively to keep someone alive, when it seems clear that their time has come), or with some forms of cosmetic surgery (on the grounds that it amounts to mutilation, or that it panders to the patient's vanity). We might sometimes find expensive treatment offensive, but usually, there, our objection is not to the treatment per se, but because it is unfairly available to the rich and not the poor: we would prefer to live in a world where everyone had access to state of the art medical care. So, then, and by and large, we think that therapy is a good thing. And yet many feel queasy about enhancement. But are therapy and enhancement really so different?

If an orthopaedic surgeon removes an osteoarthritic hip and replaces it with an implant, she will have turned back the patient's biological clock, giving him the function of a person many decades younger. Is the patient not enhancing the patient's body? Almost everyone (there will be a few exceptions, such as Christian Scientists) thinks that the operation is good, provided that we think of it as treatment of the osteoarthritis, or of the patient's mobility deficit, or of the pain caused by walking. We might even be able to live with the idea of enhancement, provided that we say that function—rather than the person himself—is enhanced. It does not seem right that the ethics of a situation should turn on a choice about how the situation is described. The reality is that the function of a hip will affect many aspects of the functioning of the whole person—including their mental state. One cannot draw a clear line between hips and bodies, or bodies and minds.

Take an intervention that would conventionally be classified as an enhancement—say the administration of oxytocin to facilitate someone's ability to bond with another. Say, for the sake of argument, that this administration has no downside (in fact oxytocin might increase bonding with one's own partner or group, but tends to increase aggression towards those not in one's own group). Can that be regarded as a therapy? For there to be a therapy there must be a pathology at which the therapy is directed. One might choose to designate the relative inability to bond prior to the administration of oxytocin, compared to the post-administration state, as a pathology. That involves making a normative claim, which seems at first blush fairly arbitrary, about what normality is.

The obvious main way in which this sort of claim might escape the stigma of arbitrariness is to say that what is normal is whatever fate deals out—whether fate uses genetics, or road traffic accidents, or family circumstances, or whatever. The problem with this is that, if adopted, it would make all medicine an attempt to change normality.

This difficulty, though, need not make us despair of all ways of policing enhancement. One might acknowledge that there is no very robust distinction between enhancement and therapy, but nonetheless seek to restrict certain types of enhancement on the grounds that they fall foul of our main ethical objections to enhancement.

7.7 Legal Regulation of Enhancement

Difficulties of definition dog any discussion of the regulation of enhancement. If enhancement and therapy are sometimes indistinguishable, one might say that the forms of enhancement that overlap with therapy are regulated by all the legislation, regulations, and other law which govern the provision of therapy.

The law permits many forms of non-therapeutic medicine and surgery: think, for instance, of breast enlargements, nose re-shaping, cosmetic dentistry, and tooth-whitening.

In relation to pre-natal enhancements (though none of the available technologies yet extends to cognitive or moral enhancements), there is tight, case-by-case basis regulation by the Human Fertilization and Embryology Authority. For that authority, the therapy/enhancement distinction, elusive though it may be, is important, and anything that might be considered to amount to an enhancement is unlikely to be licensed—making it a criminal offence to undertake it.

It is harder to make generalisations about other enhancement techniques. Coffee, a potent cognitive enhancer, is unregulated. The law does not interfere with an examination candidate's decision to have an early night's sleep (or even to take a sleeping pill) in order to optimise her performance in the examination. There is sometimes strict, but rather piecemeal, regulation of many other cognitive enhancement drugs. It is widely reported that Ritalin and similar cognitive enhancers are used by many university students to improve concentration, memory, and intellectual stamina (Bell et al. 2013; Diller 2009; Sabini and Monterosso 2005; Hildt et al. 2014; Greely et al. 2008). Most of that use will be illegal, although Ritalin and like substances can and are prescribed for conditions such as ADHD, and it might cogently be argued that we all suffer from ADHD at some times and to some degree. Parents can, if they remain within some very broad tramlines, decide how their children should be educated, and thus how their neuronal wiring is effected and affected. Although moral enhancement is commonly regarded as ethically suspect, cognitive enhancement (presuming it is not too extreme) is not similarly stigmatised. This is surely irrational. Cognitive enhancement necessarily creates an unlevel playing field: that is its whole point. The enhanced person will have financial and possibly social advantages over the unenhanced. There is also presumably some connection (which may be close or distant, depending on the facts of the case), between cognitive enhancement and moral enhancement (Pavarini et al. 2018). And when we are sleep-deprived, we are morally truncated too (Alkozei et al. 2017). Utilitarians would contend that this link is obvious and close: that morality is defined as good decision-making, and that good decision-making is, at least in part, a function of one's cognition. If your neurological software can compute faster (they say), you will be a better person. We cannot explore that contention here, and cite it only to indicate the impossibility of distinguishing neatly between cognitive enhancement and moral enhancement: to regulate one is to regulate the other, to some degree, and to leave one unregulated is to leave the other unregulated, to some degree.

Identity, though central to the debates in the literature about enhancement, does not seem to be a distinction important to the law in this context. This is unsurprising. Enhancement technologies themselves are not, as such, on the law's radar; and the law has approached questions of identity (insofar as it has recognised them at all), incoherently. It might be argued that concerns about identity lie behind the prohibitions of some illicit drugs, but if so, those concerns are empirically dubious, rarely referred to in policy documents and sentencing remarks (except in the most general terms, along the lines of 'drugs destroyed his life'), and pale into insignificance beside concerns such as public safety. We note that in the catalogue of drugs proscribed by UK law are substances such as ayahuasca whose reported effects include greater self-knowledge and *enhanced* identity (Earp 2018). When they are used traditionally as 'soul-medicine', they seem to boost rather than diminish the sense of self.

There is, then, no systematic regulation of moral enhancement technologies. There is insufficient agreement about what they are, or even whether they exist or might foreseeably exist. And without agreement about such basic matters, there can hardly be a meaningful debate about whether, and if so how, to regulate them. The law does countenance many traditional techniques of cognitive enhancement—such as education—which seem to have *some* connection, at least in some circumstances, to one's personal morality, but the endorsement seems to be endorsement by default: education may be permitted simply because it has not seriously been considered (as it might well be) to fall foul of some of the most potent and generally held objections to other types of enhancement.

7.8 Should the Law Seek to Regulate or Encourage Enhancement?

This is too big a question to ask, let alone answer, given the uncertainty about what constitutes enhancement, and particularly the doubt about where the boundary between enhancement and therapy lies.

As we have observed, the law already permits and indeed encourages in many ways (for instance by giving educational bodies charitable status) various forms of enhancement. We encourage a critical examination of that endorsement, using the ethical and legal language in which the debates about technological enhancement are carried on. It should not be presumed that simply because a practice has gone on since time immemorial, it is inoffensive. Conservatism is not argument, and viewing schooling, for instance, as a process of engineering new and permanent neuronal connections might help to focus questions about whether some forms of educational drilling are acceptable.

Having criticised that kind of conservatism, we urge another kind. There are currently too many philosophical, ethical, and scientific uncertainties about most other kinds of enhancement technologies for the law to begin to have the raw material necessary for a meaningful consideration of regulation or encouragement.

That said, we think that there are two obvious principles which should have central stage in any cautious consideration of existing or emerging technologies. The first is equality: the need to ensure a level playing field. Accordingly we consider, for instance, that the use of substances such as Ritalin to enhance intellectual and examination performance should be legally resisted. It is simply not fair on those who do not take such drugs, and it has not been demonstrated that there is a sufficient overall benefit or an insufficient overall detriment to individuals or society for their universal use to be commended. Unless all can have such drugs (and it is demonstrated conclusively that it is desirable for them to do so), none should.

The second principle relates to identity. We suspect that in the enhancement technologies of the future—and particularly the moral enhancement technologies—identity is going to be the main ethical battleground. But the specific terms of engagement in relation to the existing putative technologies are so dependent on as yet non-existent or equivocal data about most identity-changing effects that the battle cannot begin. We suggest, though, that there may be an identity-based case for the legalisation of currently unlawful substances such as psilocybin and ayahuasca, on the grounds that they are identity-enhancing. Similar observations may apply to substances typically used as antidepressants, and therefore seen as therapeutic rather than enhancing. Depression is, along with schizophrenia, a classic example of a condition that challenges the integrity of the frontier between therapy and enhancement. Depression often presents as a pathology of selfhood: it seems to erode identity. If that is right, then effective therapy will allow identity to blossom again: will allow the person to be more fully themselves again. Or perhaps the normal human condition is depressive, and the 'therapy' which alters that normal state actually enhances—with the effect of enhancing the patient's identity. But however we view depression and the chemicals and other interventions used to address it, the end result of the treatment/enhancement is the same, and the law should actively encourage the intervention. If that is right, it is hard logically (assuming that the empirical work supports identity-enhancement, and there are no outweighing downsides) not to use the law at least to permit, if not to encourage, identity-enhancing psychedelics.

One final observation. One potent argument for moral enhancement is that, even if it entails a change to the identity of the subject, it may (and particularly if combined with cognitive enhancement) help to avert great catastrophes, thus benefiting many (Persson and Savulescu 2012). We are sympathetic in principle to the utilitarian premise, but at the moment can neither see nor foresee any empirical basis for embracing technology that could do that.

The law is often criticised for lagging behind technological advance. That criticism is often just, and it would obviously be desirable, were it possible, to have in place a legal and ethical framework that accommodated, or could expand to accommodate, all possible advances. For the reasons we have explained, we do not think that is possible in the case of most enhancement technologies, and any benefit that there may be in trying is in our view outweighed by the concomitant dangers. If we try ham-fistedly to anticipate the regulatory structure that might be necessary we might well find ourselves stuck with an inadequate structure that cannot be made adequate by incremental change. Better, we think, to build that structure at the material time, from the principles that it is then apparent are the fundamental principles.

7.9 Conclusion

This chapter has considered some of the main ethical arguments for and against moral enhancement, and noted that there has, as yet, been little legislative interest in systematic regulation of the available or putative technologies. This will have to change. We have highlighted some of the criteria which will have to be considered when the change comes.

References

Alkozei A, Killgore W, Smith R, Dailey N, Bajaj S, Haack M (2017) Chronic sleep restriction increases negative implicit attitudes toward Arab Muslims. Sci Rep 7(1):1–6

Bell S, Partridge B, Lucke J, Hall W (2013) Australian university students' attitudes towards the acceptability and regulation of pharmaceuticals to improve academic performance. Neuroethics 6(1):197–205

Bublitz C (2016) Moral enhancement and mental freedom. J Appl Philos 33(1):88–106

Diller LH (2009) Running on Ritalin: a physician reflects on children, society, and performance in a pill. Bantam

Douglas T (2008) Moral enhancement. J Appl Philos 25(3):228–245

Dubljević V, Racine E (2017) Moral enhancement meets normative and empirical reality: assessing the practical feasibility of moral enhancement neurotechnologies. Bioethics 31(5):338–348

Dubljević V, Coates McCall I, Illes J (2020) Neuroenhancement at work: addressing the ethical, legal, and social implications. In: Racine G, Martineau J (eds) Organizational neuroethics. Springer, Cham, pp 87–103

Earp B (2018) Psychedelic moral enhancement. R Inst Philos Suppl 83:415–439

Earp B, Douglas T, Savulescu J (2018) Moral neuroenhancement. In: Johnson LSM, Rommelfanger KS (eds) Routledge handbook of neuroethics

Focquaert F, Schermer M (2015) Moral enhancement: do means matter morally? Neuroethics 8 (2):139–151

Greely H, Sahakian B, Harris J, Kessler R, Gazzaniga M, Campbell P, Farah M (2008) Towards responsible use of cognitive-enhancing drugs by the healthy. Nature 456(7223):702–705

Harris J (2011) Moral enhancement and freedom. Bioethics 25(2):102–111

Harris J (2016) How to be good: the possibility of moral enhancement. Oxford University Press, Oxford

Hildt E, Lieb K, Franke A (2014) Life context of pharmacological academic performance enhancement among university students–a qualitative approach. BMC Med Ethics 15(1):1–10

Pavarini G, McKeown A, Singh I (2018) Smarter than thou, holier than thou: the dynamic interplay between cognitive and moral enhancement. Front Pharmacol 9:1189–1192

Persson I, Savulescu J (2008) The perils of cognitive enhancement and the urgent imperative to enhance the moral character of humanity. J Appl Philos 25(3):162–177

Persson I, Savulescu J (2012) Unfit for the future: the need for moral enhancement. Oxford University Press, Oxford

Sabini J, Monterosso J (2005) Judgments of the fairness of using performance enhancing drugs. Ethics Behav 15(1):81–94

Sandberg A, Fabiano J (2017) Modelling the social dynamics of moral enhancement: social strategies sold over the counter and the stability of society. Camb Q Healthc Ethics 26 (3):431–445

Savulescu J, Persson I (2012) Moral enhancement, freedom and the god machine. The Monist 95 (3):399–421

Schaefer G (2015) Direct and indirect moral enhancement. Kennedy Inst Ethics J 25(3):261–289
Specker J, Focquaert F, Raus K, Sterckx S, Schermer M (2014) The ethical desirability of moral bioenhancement: a review of reasons. BMC Med Ethics 15(1):67
Wiseman H (2014) Moral enhancement— 'hard' and 'soft' forms. Am J Bioethics 14(4):48–49
Wiseman H (2016) The myth of the moral brain: the limits of moral enhancement. MIT Press, Cambridge

Chapter 8
Epilogue

Abstract This final chapter summarises the key themes of the book. It argues that a primary role of the law is facilitating and encouraging morally good behaviour. Rarely is the law in the business of *compelling* goodness. The role of law is better understood as a medium for expressing the values of society, and thereby creating a culture in which morality can grow.

Keywords Goodness · Contract · Tort · Values · Property

Does the law seek to make people good? If so:

- should it?
- how does it try?
- does it succeed?

If the law does not seek to make people good:

- should it?
- how should it try?

We have tried to address these questions by surveying large and various domains of (mostly) English law: the law of contract and the law relating to the disposition of property; the law of tort; family law; criminal law, medical law, and the (more or less non-existent) law relating to moral enhancement technologies.

We have seen that the law often aspires to improve the individual morality of citizens. Sometime it is explicit about the aspiration. That, unsurprisingly, is particularly true of public law—and particularly of criminal law.

But more often the aspiration is less obvious, and tends to be framed in the form of rules that discourage bad actions rather than encouraging good actions. Rarely, outside criminal law, family law, and the law relating to a few intentional torts, is the law much interested in mental states. In the law of contract, to be sure, there has to be an intention to create legal relations, but whether a contract has a 'moral' aim is, by and large, irrelevant. A few contracts will be struck down as contrary to public policy, but they are few and far between.

© The Author(s), under exclusive license to Springer Nature Switzerland AG 2021
C. Foster, J. Herring, *The Law as a Moral Agent*, SpringerBriefs in Law,
https://doi.org/10.1007/978-3-030-71334-8_8

This reluctance to inquire into mental states has many roots. They include the idea that a person's thoughts are sacrosanct—that thought-crime is no-crime—and the sheer evidential difficulty of such inquiries. Whatever the roots, the result is a focus on acts (and omissions). If we now consider that the law of a nation is the law of *all* the nation's inhabitants, we can begin to see why the morality generally recognised by the law has a distinct utilitarian flavour. It tends to be concerned with maximising the thriving of the greatest number—and it prosecutes that agenda by promoting (well or badly) societal stability. Even when the law is at its most stridently neoliberal (as the law of contract tends to be, except when it recognises the vulnerability of consumers) it insists that its overriding objective is peaceful cohesion and societal prosperity.

We accept that peaceful cohesion and societal prosperity are conditions in which individual morality is more likely to flourish. This is one example of morality being a collateral but desirable outcome of a legal scheme directed at something (freedom to contract) which at first blush might not seem to have much obvious moral content.

In this sense the law is, almost always, concerned with morality. It is usually concerned with creating an environment in which morality can grow; with facilitating rather than expressly fashioning or compelling morality. This, we think, is clearly a legitimate function of the law, and it is also, we contend, one of the two most effective ways in which the law can truly impinge on our moral lives. The other effective way is by declaring a society's values. Those values diffuse rapidly and deeply from an authoritative declaration in a statute or a judgment. There is a real value in having on the statute book an assertion about a fundamental value even if the statute itself is never invoked by a prosecuting authority or in a barrister's skeleton argument. *Ethos,* in other words, is hugely morally influential. Of course laws that compel or prohibit a particular course of action are potent sources of ethos-affecting declaration, but we suspect that their existence rather than their forensic muscle is what matters most.

Laws seek to embody societal norms. They inevitably have to have some moral colour, and it would be disingenuous to deny it. Explicit censure of immoral acts and omissions is important, but pales into relative insignificance beside the inchoate effect of the law's expression of a society's values.

The manufacturer's authorised representative in the EU is Springer Nature Customer Service Centre GmbH, Europaplatz 3, 69115 Heidelberg, Germany. If you have any concerns regarding our products, please contact ProductSafety@springernature.com

Printed and bound by CPI Group (UK) Ltd, Croydon, CR0 4YY
30/09/2026
02225708-0007